The Gospel
Without
Compromise

The Gospel
Without
Compromise

Catherine de Hueck Doherty

AVE MARIA PRESS
Notre Dame, Indiana 46556

Library of Congress Catalog Card Number: 75-28619

International Standard Book Number: 0-87793-104-6 (paper)
0-87793-105-4 (cloth)

Printed in the United States of America

Contents

Preface

In 1925 Pope Pius XI issued the first call to Catholic Action, calling on the laity to participate in the apostolate.

Some five years later in 1930, in Toronto, Ontario, Catherine de Hueck was one of the pioneers to respond to that call. Her personal desire was for a lone apostolate, but circumstances prevailed that made her endeavors eventuate into a group of lay people who worked for the Church in the movement known as Friendship House.

The movement evolved and grew, and in 1938 it crossed the border to the United States and entered the field of the interracial apostolate in Harlem and elsewhere. In 1947, subsequent to her marriage with the late Eddie Doherty, a well-known journalist, Catherine returned to Canada to establish the Madonna House Apostolate in Combermere, Ontario.

During all these years her voice and her pen spoke out. In lectures and talks up and down the North American continent, and in a ceaselessly flowing river of articles, letters and books, she penetrated the lives of Christians with the unwavering message of the necessity of living the gospel. A generation of priests, sisters and lay people in the 1950's was nourished and sustained by her ideas in books such as *Dear Sister, Dear Seminarian, Where Love Is God Is* and *My Russian Yesterdays.*

Her Russian origin and training, the trauma of the Russian revolution, the sudden change from riches to destitution, the living experience of being a menial worker—all brought home to Catherine, in a deep and profound fashion, the value and the truth of the gospel message.

I met Catherine in 1950, and some months later became her spiritual director. For the past quarter of a century I have lived and worked with her on a daily basis. I am in a position to state from my own personal experience that she has lived the title of this book, *The Gospel Without Compromise.*

This steadfast Christian woman views the gospel—Christ and his words—as Good News. She insists and reaffirms that the core of the Good News is God's love for us. She exemplifies in her life not only the Lord's commandments, but also his counsels of poverty, chastity and obedience.

She writes in the introduction: "I shall not discuss directly the many controversies which are ebbing and flowing all around us today. Instead, I will try to present to my readers, from a hundred different directions, the Good News. The Good News is God's love for us, and his one great commandment is to love. If we are living that commandment and not just rendering lip service to it, we shall change the face of economics, politics, technology and anything else which needs to be changed."

I think Catherine's presentation of the Good News, if lived out, will not only change the face of economics, politics and technology, but will change the readers' hearts as well, if they too accept the gospel without compromise.

Rev. John T. Callahan
Madonna House
Combermere, Ontario

Introduction

The world of man is in turmoil. It has been in turmoil before, but this turmoil, this confusion is a new type. It is a turmoil and confusion of the minds and souls of men who are searching for the true answer to their existence, God.

One of the reasons for this turmoil is the development of science and technology, the discovery of new universes, the entry of man into space, limitless space. He has set out to conquer space with his instruments, but his instruments are conquering him. It almost seems that the more man comes to know about the world in which he lives, the less he understands about himself.

There was a time when he thought he was the center of his universe. Now, beholding the immensity which surrounds him, he seems to have shrunk into utter insignificance. He feels fragmented. There seems to be no meaning to his life, no sense, so he fashions a thousand idols for himself in order to find temporary peace, psychological peace, by worshiping them.

But no sooner has he completed his idol—be it status, wealth, sex, or power—than he finds it is mere sawdust under his feet. Man rises in search of yet another idol, until he comes to the ultimate of all idols, himself. Yet, even this cannot satisfy him. And so, restless, he begins again to search for the God that he doesn't really believe has died after all.

He cannot see, of course, that already the living God is leading him, as he led humanity from the very first day of creation, into the truth. In one sense, God *is* dying, that is, the wrong conceptions that men have had of God for centuries. The true God is rising from the ashes of that death in his new splendor. It will be a splendor of truth that modern man can understand, a splendor of love that modern man seeks so desperately. It will be in a splendor of humility and meekness on his part, for deep down man does want to understand, to grasp, to possess God.

In the midst of this confusion, this turmoil, the Holy Spirit once more descends with his pentecostal fire. In the ancient city of Rome, 2,000 men of God gathered to make the gospel of the resurrected and eternally resurrecting Christ relevant to the secular, confused, frightened, idol-making man of the streets of our cities. Vatican Council II called not only Catholics but all men of goodwill to reexamine their consciences, to reexamine their relationships with the humble, Suffering Servant, our Lord Jesus Christ.

The Council called all Christians to preach the gospel to all men everywhere. Not in order to convert them to some particular church, but in order to bring them the face of Love, the face of God, *by preaching the gospel with their lives.* This is the cry of the Church, the cry of the bishops to their people, and to all men on earth. For all men are loved by God, and all men are called to love God back, each according to his conscience, each according to his knowledge of the face of God.

But to the Catholic, the Council enjoins the special task of penetrating the secular world, tenderly, lovingly, by putting this gospel message into their political, economic and everyday lives.

This is the essence of the Church's message to the Catholic world. It is a tremendous message, one that can bring the light of Christ into the darkest corner of our fragmented, confused, searching, angry and frightened world. But it demands of us that we put aside all nonessentials, that we stop all the word games, all the useless discussions. Yes, we must now come to the essence of things.

The essence is very simple: We must begin to live by *faith,* and not by mere "religion." We must have an encounter with God and allow him to enter into our very depths. We must remember that God loved us *first*, and that our religion is truly a love affair between God and man, man and God; it is not merely a system of morals and dogmas.

We must love God back, passionately! How? Through the *other*. We must love our neighbor, not only as ourselves but with the heart of God. Christ said to his disciples, "By this shall men know that you are my disciples, that you love one another *as I have loved you.*"

To love with the heart of God we must empty ourselves totally of self. We must empty ourselves of self, so as to allow Christ to love through us. Without him we cannot love anything or anyone, not even ourselves.

In order to show the face of Love to others, in order to empty ourselves so that Love will shine in our business emporiums, our stock exchanges, in our suburban residential areas, we must become poor ourselves. Not even poverty of spirit, which means that we realize how utterly dependent we are on God, is enough. We must be poor in the reality of daily life.

This is no time for Christians to be buying $100,000 homes. This is no time for worrying about our "images." This is no time for religious orders to be building million-dollar plants and $75,000 altars. (I am not suggesting we become paupers!) It is simply a time to become poor, to give to others of our surplus, yes, but also of our necessity. Can we not live normally and curb our unruly desires for a thousand unnecessary gadgets and status symbols?

This is the time for becoming Christians in the fullness of that simple phrase: "followers of Christ." To each and every one of us, no matter what our state of life, Christ's life stands as our example. All we have to do is translate it for all to understand.

Only love can do this. The father of love is faith. We must begin to live by faith of which the outward signs of religion are but handmaidens, and of which the sacraments are the visible signs. We must truly plunge into the scriptures and the liturgy. The Word will illumine us. The Tremendous Lover will feed us with himself and give us the strength and the grace to love as he loved.

You will not find in these pages any discussion of the great problems of the times. These themes, these tragedies, these happenings are well covered by the secular and Christian press across the land. My intention is to approach these problems on a different level.

First, we must truly enter into the agony of these events, into the anguish connected with them. This demands a constant prayer for an increase of faith. Much of the world believes that God is dead, and perhaps just as many couldn't care one way or another whether he is dead or alive. In prayer we remember that God does not want sacrifice, but love and mercy. So we pray for faith and realize that the desperate conditions of the world demand that we should become a holocaust, a sacrifice to the Lord.

No, I shall not discuss directly the many controversies which are ebbing and flowing all around us today. Instead, I will try to present to my readers, from a hundred different directions, the Good News. The Good News is God's love for us, and his one great commandment is to love. If we are living that commandment and not just rendering lip service to it, we shall change the face of economics, politics, technology and anything else which needs to be changed.

This book contains some of my writings over a period of years. Each section may be read and reflected upon separately, although I believe there is a theme which unites them all: the commandment of love. As you read on, you will hear that same refrain repeated over and over again—like a child repeats a nursery rhyme. I don't believe it is childish, however, but childlike. After all, the Lord said that unless we become like children we cannot enter his kingdom. My prayer has always been, "Lord, give me the heart of a child, and the awesome courage to live it out."

If we have the courage to live a life of love with the hearts of children, the world will change. The world will change if we have the courage and the love to live the gospel without compromise.

Chapter 1 / *Troubled Times*

The Trouble With Christians

There is no denying that I am a modern traveler. One time when I was out visiting our other houses, I traveled around the world twice according to air miles. Everywhere I went—hotels, restaurants, pubs, cocktail lounges, humble Negro huts, rich Italian palaces, American and European suburban homes—everywhere my impression was that there is one main topic of conversation in our day and age. That topic is *God*.

Be he dead or alive, he preoccupies men's minds with his strange and eternal fascination. Do people deny him? They cannot do it calmly. Do they accept him? They accept him often with great passion. But alas, in most instances, those who say they believe in him are somewhat lukewarm and far from passionate in their argumentation, as if they were not quite sure of themselves. There is no dynamism, no pentecostal fire burning in them.

Yes, my deepest impression from my travels was that man's hunger for God is at its peak, but that Christians do not know how to fill this hunger. Maybe it's because they do not *recognize* this hunger for what it is, and thus do not realize how to fill it.

But let's face it. If the world is atheistic, if much of it has not yet heard the Good News, or if it has heard but not accepted it, then the main fault lies with us Christians who have not lived the gospel. We have only filled the libraries of the world with books which have more or less watered down the message of the gospel.

Christianity has become an affair of ethical, moral behavior. An affair of going to Church, of learning rules to make sure that one will get to heaven. The gap between the reality of the gospel and the teaching contained in all those library volumes has reaped its harvest of damage.

My impression from traveling was that the world is crying for the Bread of Life, for the Living Waters that Christ promised—in fact, for God himself. But Christians who possess the bread and the water do not know how to share the bread they eat. They forget that whoever eats the bread of the Lord must be truly "eaten up" by others. Having received Love, the Christian should give love.

My impressions were that few Christians were in love with God, and fewer yet realized that he was in love with them. So the voice of those who say that "God is dead" is louder than the voice of those who say that he is alive.

We should stop talking about God and start living out the gospel in our lives, manifesting the image of the Lord so clearly in our hearts that no one can possibly say that he is dead. We should stop worrying about theological theory and begin building among ourselves communities of love.

We live in pentecostal times. Once again the invincible love of the Holy Spirit is among us. We have only to open our hearts to it and we shall change the world. Then our own hearts will contain the fire and flame that Jesus sent to renew the earth.

When the apostles went to preach the Good News and to baptize as the Lord instructed them, they didn't have any catechetical manuals. They had the gospel. They had the Holy Spirit. They brought the kingdom of Christ to an immense portion of the then-known world.

Why can't we modern Christians adopt the "techniques" of the apostles and of the early Christians? True, we may wind up in some prisons, prisons of rejection, ridicule and maybe even physical prisons.

We may be crucified in a thousand ways, maybe even locked up in psychiatric wards as St. Francis might be if he were alive today. But so what? The gospel would be preached to the poor and the kingdom of God would begin at least to have a toehold in our modern world. Yes, Jesus came to cast fire on the earth. Would that this fire were enkindled in our hearts today!

Age of Paradoxes

There is a hunger for God. Perhaps our communistic, atheistic, secularistic, pragmatic, neopagan era will be known to history as the era of man's *hunger for God.* There is a hunger for the Absolute, for the God of truth, for the Christ of the gospels.

For us who live in this era it is difficult to see ourselves objectively and in the right perspective. Contradictions and paradoxes abound. Extremes confront each other.

In Russia, officially an atheistic country, over 100 young men entered one of the few remaining seminaries. These young people have been exposed to atheism from their youth. A Russian theologian who returned from Russia says that religion and interest in it dominate Russian youth in many ways.

In California, topless waitresses serve in restaurants; not too far away hermitages are built on the mountaintops. People in great numbers flock to both.

The hippies disturb the consciences of the older generation. They appear, like St. Francis once appeared on the scene of the world. They stir something deep in men's hearts even though their witness is marred with love-ins and drugs. They still make the adults around them uncomfortable for reasons other than the latter.

Across the nations the cry for peace rises from the lips of the young and old alike. Mature men with good positions in government ask themselves if they can continue at their posts while their decisions involve contracts for napalm and the buying of new and deadly weapons.

Millions seek the answer for the hunger in their hearts in various Oriental cults. Young people are turning to Kierkegaard, Bonhoeffer and Teilhard de Chardin for their nourishment.

Catholics, Protestants and Jews are returning to the sources of their faith in their scriptures. Some men are burying Christ, and some are studying him. Men are both bothered by him and cannot leave him alone.

The barque of St. Peter is rocked by men trying to arrive at essential truths but often getting sidetracked along the road.

Many more "civilized" people in the West are considering birth control, while "primitive" peoples refuse it. Celibacy is becoming more of a problem for Western clergy, while Russian priests who are married before receiving the diaconate petition for celibacy. In a country where many dedicated communists embrace celibacy to witness to their cause, these priests wonder why they shouldn't witness to the Parousia and to the living God!

Paradoxes! Confusion! Searching! All these accompany any search for the Absolute. Such are the signs of our times. Who will assuage this hunger? How will we answer this search for the Absolute? Who will listen to the silent voice within man's heart? On this listening depends human history and the very existence of our planet.

False Deification of Man

What name shall we put on the times in which we live? Neopagan? Yet, many people we call pagan sometimes teach us the ways of peace, love and truth! Is it a time of "preevangelization"? There have been such pregospel times before, but then people believed in some gods and paid their respects to them.

Whatever label we want to put on these times, we of the West who have heard the gospel have certainly not *incarnated* the teaching of Christ in whom we profess to believe.

Is it possible that we live in times when the average man is a little god unto himself? If so, we are back to the days of the tower of Babel. Perhaps this is why in this age of great technological advancement in methods of communication, we are less capable of communicating with one another as individuals and as nations.

Whatever era we are living in—however we tend to describe it—it is truly a frightening era. It is an era of immense contrasts. Technologically, we have reached supreme heights. We have almost conquered space and time. But in the process, we are destroying nature and ourselves. Earth, planets, water and air are being polluted. As we conquer space and time we are destroying our planet. By traveling faster, and by having invented a million gadgets that save us time, we must now turn to psychiatrists to find out what to do with it!

Our technological miracles have brought in their wake fears that we never knew about before. We have nightmares of becoming robots and mere extensions of machines. We feel dehumanized. We are not sure anymore who we are, and we seek our identity again in the soundproof offices of psychologists and psychiatrists.

We are filled with guilt because the very means of communication we have invented are opening our eyes to the tragic mess that we who think we are gods have made of the world. We cannot sleep as peacefully as we did before because the poverty of our brethren is brought into our living room on a small screen—piped in vividly and realistically!

How long will we be able to live in the polluted air that we have created? How long can we live amid the deafening noise of our cities with news of violence, death and tragedy?

What era are we living in? It is an era of the deification of the self. Isn't it time that we fall on our knees and, turning once again to the only true God that we half-believe in, ask him to make us clean from the leprosy of mind and heart? Then we may well begin another era. An era of love and of peace.

Fragmented Man

Modern man is a fragmented being. Psychiatrists call it schizophrenia, or some other big scientific name. True, one can safely say that modern man is divided within himself, a split personality of some kind. He is emotionally disturbed, afraid of taking responsibilities, of facing life. This fear of responsibilty is especially frightening in our technological age, already so insecure with hot and cold wars and threats of nuclear war hanging overhead.

A partial cause of this fragmentation, of this division within himself, is his rejection of all the ways of old, of much of the wisdom of the past. Frightened and impatient, he wants to shake off all shackles that seem to bind him. Any kind of authority appears to him as a shackle which impedes his free movements. He feels like a Gulliver, tied with a thousand strings by his ancestors whom he looks upon as ignorant little pygmies.

Modern man is excited and enamored of any new machine that will help him escape from reality, which will help him speed to some "better place." Actually, he goes nowhere, only to return to where he started. Many technological advancements and gadgets only fragment him further. He has recourse to psychiatry and psychology to put himself back together again. But all they do is perhaps give him some insight into himself and his emotional patterns; then they ask him to use his own resources to make himself whole.

But he can't. He needs more than science. He needs God. If he would arise and go in search of God, he would find the wholeness he seeks.

In the bible, the word of God, is the advice and the direction that would begin to make him whole: "Oh, children, how long will you love childishness and desire those things which are harmful to yourselves? How long will you hate knowledge?" (Prv 1:22). "You have despised all my counsels and have neglected my reprehensions" (1:25). "Be not afraid of sudden fear, nor of the power of the wicked falling upon you. For the Lord will be at your side and will keep your foot so that you will not be taken" (3:25-26). "For I also was my father's son, tender and as an only son in the sight of my mother. And he taught me and said, 'Let your heart receive my word.' . . . Hear, oh my son, and receive my words, that years of life may be multiplied for you" (4:3, 10).

Out of this book of Proverbs comes the wisdom that our modern world needs. In other passages of the same book the writer advises men to absorb the wisdom of their fathers and their ancestors, and then to add his own to it and pass it on to their own sons.

Much of the fragmentation of modern man, of his split personality, could be healed if man followed the advice of Proverbs. If each generation preserved the wisdom of the past, added to it by prayer, fasting and true living, then passed this treasure on to its sons, there would always be a harmonious blending of the old and the new.

What we need is the wisdom of God much more than that of psychiatry and science. God's wisdom would lead us to wholeness even in our atomic age. Yes, we must put away "our love for childishness." We must stop being fools who desire what is harmful for us. We must cease to hate true knowledge, true wisdom, which is God himself, and begin earnestly to search for it. We must become childlike in order to be fully mature, grown-up and responsible people, in truth a kingly people, a priestly people, a holy people, the people of God.

Key to Loneliness

Do we realize how utterly, tragically lonely man is, especially in our Western world? The only way we can unlock and set free this loneliness which cries out for help at the top of its voice in a most profound silence is to use the key of love.

All around and about us is constant talk about poverty. Learned theologians discuss it in words that escape most of us. Philosophers do likewise. The elite, wherever they are, whoever they are, make it a conversation piece constantly. The young never cease talking about it.

But in all these conversations no one dares to look into himself and behold his loneliness. For who among us these days isn't lonely? Do not the theologians, the philosophers, the elite, the young also feel this loneliness? Of course. We are all lonely, those on the top of the human heap, those in the middle, and those below. Yet the answer to all this loneliness is so evident, so simple, so direct.

True, we must share our goods, our physical goods, and many of us do, or try to. But have we forgotten that "man does not live by bread alone," and that it is that very dimension of love that we are reluctant to give our neighbor? For loneliness has a door and we, each one of us, have the key to it. The key is acceptance of the other, without questions. Acceptance makes the other realize that he is loved, and because we have given him our love we can now give him the fruit of love—tenderness, compassion, gentleness and understanding.

Yes, yes, we have the key to the loneliness of the "other," and the other has the key to my loneliness. The only thing we have to do is insert it into the keyhole of our hearts, open the door, and enter. But we are afraid, because this means a deep, loving involvement with the other. We prefer to be involved perhaps in the ghetto or in some other place of our own choosing where we don't have to use keys to one another's hearts. We only have to use *words* there, poor symbols of the key we leave unused.

It's time now. It's high time for us to understand that we must use that key. We must enter each other's hearts, and we must do so without fear.

Yes, we have to go into the depths of men's hearts. We have to go there without fears, for God will be there. He will teach us how to dispel the terrible loneliness that grips men these strange and tragic days. For unless we really begin to understand that *not by bread alone does man live,* we shall perish.

Christians, growing in wisdom and grace in the school of God's love, know this loneliness of men perhaps better than anyone else. They see it in the eyes of priests, in the eyes of bewildered religious, in the eyes of husbands, wives, parents, young people, the poor, yes, and in the eyes of the rich.

Loneliness holds the men of our age and times in a grip that seems unbreakable. Yet, it can be broken! It can be broken by love, a love offered silently and gently from one human heart to another.

Or it might be a love expressed in words, but these words must come from a heart united with God in the quiet prayer of contemplation. Neither is it enough for Christians to simply love. They must love with the very heart of Christ himself.

In order to do so we must open our hearts to humanity. We must take upon ourselves the pain of every man as Christ did. We must identify ourselves constantly with the lonely ones; we must share their loneliness. We must die to self. Then Christ will live in us and love in us. In the face of such love loneliness will depart and our world will be able to gather itself. The islands will merge into a mainland—the one body of Christ.

Worthless People?

One of the greatest tragedies of our times is the loss of our identity, especially among the young. It is a loss of identity that seems to be accompanied by an inability to love and accept oneself.

Thousands of young people pass through Madonna House every year. The majority suffer both from this loss of identity and from their inability to love themselves as they are. Could it be that we still have not taught the gospel to them as we should have?

For the gospel can be summed up in two commandments of love: Love God . . . love your neighbor *as yourself.* Christians, young, old and in between, must understand that one can love neither God nor one's neighbor unless one loves oneself and accepts oneself as being unique, irreplaceable, beloved by the God who created us.

God loves us—not because we are good, but because *he* is good! But it may also be that we cannot accept ourselves because the yardstick with which we measure ourselves is our *ability to produce,* our "production quotient." We think we are worth what we can produce. Our society, culture, mores—all seem to gang up on us from childhood to give us this yardstick and to make us believe in it.

Salaries are raised in the business world according to our production: How many items have we sold? How many orders have we brought in? What were our grades in class? How many insurance policies did we sell? And on and on.

We measure ourselves as if we were extensions of machines instead of human beings. Failures are reprehensible. No one seems to realize that without failures there can be no successes. Failures are stepping-stones to success, even in the natural order of things.

This mentality blinds us to our true value. The incarnation, death and resurrection of Christ are the measure of our true value. We are worth three hours' agony on the cross. More, we are worth Jesus' whole life. "For the Father so loved the world that he gave his only Son."

Yes, this is our worth. But modern men, especially modern youth, do not seem to realize this. They reject themselves and thus alienate themselves from God and from their neighbors.

What is to be done about this situation which makes psychiatrists rich and leaves everyone else poor and sick? *The answer is to preach the gospel with one's life.* Let there arise among us people who, falling in love with God, will be able to show God's love to all who think they are unlovable and cannot accept even themselves.

If all those who suffer from an identity crisis could see Christ's love shine in the eyes of a Christian, they would be healed. Love would be let loose in the world. Christ would become visible again.

The Deepest Hunger

Everywhere, all over the world, a new hunger has arisen. A hunger for God. Everywhere across the world, man tries to satisfy this hunger. Yet, in some undefinable manner, the hunger persists. We see the extraordinary phenomenon of a stream of pilgrims moving back and forth across the breadth of the world.

How can this hunger be assuaged? The answer is simple: *by a love that is face to face, person to person.*

Men these days are teetering on the edge of an abyss, with the threat of nuclear war as a background. Man is bewildered by the greed, the insatiable greed of the military complex. He is beginning to find intolerable the monotony of the assembly line that kills his spirit. The bewilderment continues with the rape of a world which offers air-conditioning and other comforts while shortening, as a whole, the life of the human species.

These and many other questions have coalesced into one question: Who is God? Man is slowly beginning to understand that only from him and only by living his rules of love will the problems of our tragic days be solved.

This is the moment, then, when we who call ourselves Christians must face one another, for the allaying of man's hunger begins by man facing man on a one-to-one basis. To begin to assuage this hunger, man must understand that he is loved, loved as a friend, loved as a brother in Christ. It must be done person to person. It cannot be done *en masse*.

It is only in the eyes of another, in the face of another, that man can find the Icon of Christ. There are many ways of praising God, many ways of praying to him, many ways of searching for him. But today there is one great way, one profound way, one gentle, tender and compassionate way. It is by a person-to-person love. We must make the other aware that we love him. If we do, he will know that God loves him. When he knows that God loves him, he will cease to hunger. He will know that God has prepared a table for him and has invited him to come to his feast, to drink his wine, and to eat the bread which is himself.

He who participates in the Eucharistic Sacrifice, having been brought there by someone else, will know what love is. He will never hunger again. He will understand, in an incredible way, how much he is loved.

The World Is Cold

Charity is dying and the world is cold. The only heat that may really warm it for a second before it destroys itself may be the heat from the atomic bomb!

Charity is dying and the world is cold, cold with hatred of brother toward brother. In many parts of the world men kill men like themselves, and again the earth cries out in fear and trembling and abhorrence at having to absorb once more the blood shed by Cain.

Charity is dying and the world is cold. Cold with suspicion and doubt. Men walk in dark fogs that seem to rise from nowhere but in reality are everywhere. Fogs distort reality, and make the real seem unreal. They bring suspicion and doubt because they bring fear.

Charity is dying and the world is cold. Cold with fears, fears that bring suspicion and confusion. Fears that block out the intellect and imagination and make people neurotic and psychotic.

All this is happening because charity is dying. But why is charity dying? What is charity? Charity is love, and love is a Person, love is God. Is God dying? Yes, God is always dying when men keep on crucifying him in his Mystical Body.

But charity is also dying in the hearts of men because they refuse the love of God. In fact, they refuse God himself. They reject him. They say they do not need him. They say they can live without him. Or they say he does not exist, that he never existed. They say he was simply a legend, some archetype of primitive societies discovered in the psychiatrist's office. They say he was simply an opiate concocted by the ruling classes to keep the poor poorer and the downtrodden more downtrodden.

Christ perhaps is still being crucified in his Mystical Body, but Alleluia, he is alive! He was raised from the dead! He is God, and he lives in us and will continue to love us until our last breath, no matter how we feel about him.

The Sacred Heart of Christ reigns supreme over men, over all the world of creatures, over all the universes that man has or will discover. The Galilean will conquer again and again and again.

Charity too can be resurrected in the hearts of men if only they will stop and think about Love, about God, about the incredible and true fact that *God loved them first, and that all they have to do to banish strife, wars, atomic bombs, suspicions, doubts and fears, is to begin to love him back—and all their brothers.*

Then the light and fire of charity will be so immense that no one will have to fear either atomic bombs or the hatred of his brother.

Lord, Have Mercy!

Lord, have mercy . . .

Let my prayer rise like incense before you . . . for the living dead! The ones who, with their lips, profess their creed of love, and call themselves your followers but, in action, deny both love and you.

Lord, have mercy . . .

Let my prayer rise like incense before you . . . for the living dead who should be on fire with the zeal of your Father's house, but who are sound asleep, indifferent to the pain, injustice, sorrow and useless death suffered by their fellowmen, their brothers and sisters in you.

Lord, have mercy . . .

Let my prayer rise like incense before you . . . for the living dead who walk the earth preaching hatred between races and nations . . . preaching violence, and executing its dark deeds, yet worshiping you on the Sabbath Day.

Lord, have mercy . . .

Let my prayer rise like incense before you . . . for the living dead who, holding positions of trust and honor, betray both, even while they swear "to speak the truth and nothing but the truth" and, in so doing, crucify you who are Truth.

Lord, have mercy . . .

Let my prayer rise like incense before you . . . for the living dead who, having so many possessions, seek more and get them at whatever cost, by threats, exploitation, injustice, coercion and sheer brutal force, while showing themselves publicly in the front pews of your churches.

Lord, have mercy . . .

Let my prayer rise like incense before you . . . for the faithful departed, for they were faithful to you and to us.

The Specter of Fear

Fear has come to dwell in the world. Its immense shadow has entered the halls of government and the minds of those who govern. Like a dark mist, fear has seeped into every nook and corner of the world. It has come to dwell in palaces and in hovels; in farmhouses and city apartments it is at home. It has made its home too in the hearts of the poor of the world who have no roof over their heads. No one is exempt from its influence.

Fear is the child of hate and of ignorance and of prejudice. It cannot stand the light of love, of peace and of truth. Why have we allowed our days to be filled with fear-begetting thoughts and actions? Communism could not have found a fertile soil for its hates to grow in if we had not prepared that soil in some strange fashion.

Could it be that we have refused to love? Could it be that we have rendered love lip service only? Could it be that we have allowed our ignorance and our prejudice to blot the face of Love in our brethren? How else could fear come to dwell with us and hang over us like a mist blurring the vision between man and man?

We must cast out fear or we shall perish. Already we are asking questions which only fear could have made us ask. People wanted to know a while ago what they should do (morally!) if, when they were snug in their bomb shelter, others came knocking who were also in need of shelter. A strange question indeed for Christians to ask, or anyone who says he believes in God.

Across the centuries a gentle voice is still heard in the land: "Greater love has no man than he lay down his life for his friends." Perfect love casts out fear. Perfect love lays down its life. Have we forgotten about this? It seems we have.

We had better remember before it is too late, and before fear has bound us with its strong and ominous ropes—before we really die the death of our souls. For if we allow fear to dominate us, then, indeed, those who have the power to kill our bodies will also have the power to kill our souls, and we shall have given them that power.

Let us begin to love. Let us turn our face to God. Let us not ask questions about shelters but simply take it for granted that we will share it with those who haven't got one, or who are in greater need. Let us begin to live the gospel without compromise, and fear will be cast out. Love will come to reign and we might yet experience its fruit—peace. Our fallout shelters might yet become simple storage rooms, or, better yet, children's playrooms. Places of life and not strongholds against death.

The Modern Slaying of Abel

God asked Cain where his brother Abel was. And Cain answered, "Am I my brother's keeper?" To how many of us today could God address the same question, and how many of us might give the same answer? Cain slew his brother because he envied him. We kill our brothers, slowly, deliberately, almost with malice aforethought. This is not because we, the affluent nations, envy other people. No. We have left them in a state where no one can really envy them. No. We are killing, meting out death, not because of envy, but because of avarice and greed.

We have given mere pennies for the raw materials of poor nations and charged dollars for the processed goods. We knew full well that without "purchase pennies" their standard of living would not improve, and slowly, through much misery and pain, they would come to death by starvation. Then we would put on the mask of charity, benignly bestowing a few million, or even billions that we could easily afford but which would not solve their pain, nor alleviate their misery.

Am I my brother's keeper? If we truly examined our Western conscience—the conscience of the so-called affluent society—we would be trembling indeed. It would be clear that we have slain our brother by enlarging our profits. Our profits! That is all we care about these days. Thousands of death-dealing planes and weapons of all kinds are being sold by most of the "affluent societies" to the countries of the Middle East. We are delighted, because they prolong our own lives while the lives of others are destroyed in endless skirmishes and wars all over the world.

Am I my brother's keeper? Oh no! I am my brother's killer! It is a wonder that anyone employed in the making of these munitions, from the president of the company down to the man who sweeps up at night, can look at their faces in the mirror or go to church on Sundays.

No wonder we are caught in the net of our own guilt. It is a strange guilt. It is born of our inordinate desire for the good things of life, for a style of life that is almost barbarous in its hedonism. This begets a kind of guilt which does not allow the individual to be at peace with God, his fellowman, or even with himself.

Am I my brother's keeper? No! But at long last my brothers of the poor nations are slowly gathering, gathering to face us. The confrontation will be terrible. For as we look at this incredibly immense gathering of our poor brothers (whom we have exploited to the limit of anybody's endurance), they will suddenly turn into the figure of Christ—all of them—a Christ armed with cords. He will chase us, the traffickers in his temple, the moneylenders, the death-sellers, with the cords of his wrath which we so justly deserve.

Am I my brother's keeper? This is the question we have to ask. On our answer hinges our political, economic and individual survival.

A Time for Stillness

People walk around in fear—psychological fear, spiritual fear, intellectual fear. Men look around and hear on all sides the explosion of bombs. They go to sleep wondering if their cities will be attacked. People are afraid to travel by air, by train, or by almost any means of transportation. There is constantly the fear of something going wrong.

Fear puts deep and tragic roots into the hearts of men. With fear comes doubt. Look at all the bombings and destructions! How can I believe in a God who would permit such things? Extreme doubt, like a poisonous flower, comes forth. No one remembers that his God is tender, compassionate, understanding, forgiving. Nobody stops to think that God did not start the bombing, did not hijack the planes, did not kill or maim people in wars. There is a strange aggressiveness in us which blames God for these things. Perhaps it is begotten by the doubts, the fear, the near-madness that surrounds us today on all sides.

This is the time for stillness. Stand still and listen so that you can get perspective on your life according to God's plan. Everywhere people are grabbing, grabbing. Nobody feels he should do anything for anybody. Grabbing is avarice: "This is *our* gold, *our* oil, *our* electricity." Instead of using the word "we" you hear everywhere the word "I." When nations and individuals reach that stage, they will fall apart, because the greatest sin before God is pride; avarice is its handmaid. To grab for myself that which belongs to all is a grave and tragic sin.

Now, over the whole world, whether we know it or not, the strange pall of sin falls like a dark fog, and we are walking through it. No wonder we are full of fears. The answer, again, is to stand still and listen, and God will blow the fog away if we let him. We must all be convinced that what he has told us—that we must really love one another—alone can bring about the salvation of the world.

Such a very simple thing, and yet such a profound thing. As soon as we stand still and listen we shall sense as well as hear what our heart is saying, for this is the age of the heart and not of conceptual thinking. Stand still and listen to what the heart says. As soon as we do that and realize that my brother is my joy, that my brother is my life, fear will fall away from us. We will meet each other again; the smog will have cleared away.

As we meet each other, we will meet Christ, for in each one is Christ: The Lord is in *our* midst. As we look into each other's eyes we shall see his eyes, as when we look into the eyes of the icons. In those eyes we shall see tenderness beyond all understanding, a tenderness which can only be absorbed by the heart. There we shall see a compassion that will embrace us like a warm mantle on a cold day. There we shall see a gentleness, the gentleness of a mother's arms enfolding a child.

Having looked at the face of Jesus we shall suddenly exclaim: "Father, I have found you!" For we can find the Father only through the Son. He is the road to the Father but, strange as it might sound, you have to stand still and listen. When the smog and the fog have been blown away, then into your heart will come peace. Then you will understand that by following Christ with the help of the Holy Spirit, you shall enter into the heart of the Father, for which you have been destined since birth.

It's all so very simple! How many of us are afraid, how many of us are lonely! If so, stand still and listen. The voice of the Lord will speak to our hearts. Little by little our eyes will meet the eyes of God, and we will know compassion, love and tenderness. If we accept it, we must pass it on to our neighbor. That is the way peace will reign on earth. But if you or I are going to imitate the ways of the nations, there will be no peace. There will only be darkness, tragedy, more fears and more wars.

We stand on a very narrow edge today. Which way are we going to move? Along the edge of faith, hope and love? This is the path God gives us when we listen. On either side is an abyss. Which are we going to choose? It's up to us. This is the hour of choosing. May it be the hour of standing still, the hour of listening, the hour of prayer.

Chapter 2 / Church & Council

The Council's Clear Message

"The joys and the hopes, the griefs and the anxieties of the men of this age, especially those who are poor or in any way afflicted, these too are the joys and hopes, the griefs and the anxieties of the followers of Christ."

The above quote is taken from the *Pastoral Constitution on the Church in the Modern World* and its introductory statement.

Will it take a lifetime, or only a moment, to understand that in those few words, in that short sentence, are really contained all the Second Vatican Council had to say to the people of God and to all humanity? No mere man or group of men wrote that statement. It is a pentecostal statement. The Holy Spirit inspired it, and the Pope and the bishops—praise be to God, the Lord of creation!—had hearts open enough, minds and souls ready enough to accept the prompting of the Holy Spirit, and to give it to us. Now it is up to us, the people of God, the followers of Christ.

Once more, in language so clear that a third-grader can understand it, we have restated for us the essence of the gospel from which our bourgeois mentality has been shrinking away. Alas, our theologians and moralists have fostered this slipping away through hair-splitting arguments and by stressing the letter instead of the spirit of the law. We have forgotten the stark sight of a man crucified on a small hill in Palestine, a man who was also God, and who gave us a simple, uncompromising message: *By this shall all men know that you are my disciples, that you love one another AS I HAVE LOVED YOU.*

How else can we make our own the joys, hopes, griefs and anxieties of the men of our age, all those who are poor or in any way afflicted, unless we love others as Christ loved us? If we don't, we have no right to call ourselves "followers of Christ," or "Christians." It is because we do call ourselves such and do not act out and incarnate the gospel in our lives that we have become a scandal to our brothers. Are these harsh words, or words of anger or hostility? They are words of anguish, of anxiety, of pain beyond words!

Looking at the affluent world of the United States and Canada from the depths of its Harlems and its slums, and with the eyes of the silent poor, my heart cries out in agony. The middle-of-the-road Christian does not understand that love serves, that it is color-blind, that it knows no difference of race and creed, that it bypasses the differences of language, culture and status. We must love with the heart of Christ or not at all.

So what are all those endless discussions about housing, civil rights, about this way or that way to help the poor, about the pros and cons of poverty programs? How far we are from those quoted introductory words of the Council document! We have not yet taken upon ourselves the griefs, the joys, the sorrows of all men. We have not yet learned to love with our own hearts, let alone with the heart of Christ.

"If a man asks you for your coat, give him your jacket too," says the gospel. We bicker about wheat for poor countries, about money needed for the transportation of that wheat when we should mortgage our houses, if need be, to help our neighbor. We walk in fear, and we walk in guilt because we're already before the judgment seat of God. Under the neon lights in our urban centers we toss and turn in our beds, unable to sleep even with all our pills. Why? Because deep down within us we know that we have not allowed Christ to live in our suburbs. We know that we have kept him out of jobs because he is a Negro or Puerto Rican or some other sort of "undesirable."

Yes, tranquilizers have ceased to tranquilize us because our consciences already stand before the all-seeing eye of God. We know we have too much to eat, too much to drink. We spend too much money on "good times" which turn out to be nightmares because the faces of hungry people of the world haunt our bedrooms. Neither our soft background music nor our electric blankets pacify us because we dream of women giving birth to children on dusty and filthy streets around the world.

The choice is clear: Either we love with the heart of Christ, or we die a strange death of being lifeless robots. Yes, that opening sentence of the Council's document is another call of the loving Christ through the Holy Spirit for us to awaken and become real Christians.

From Catholics to Christians

We Catholics must become Christians. We must have a personal confrontation with God and with his help solve our crises of faith. For it is in this realm that everything begins. Unless this personal dimension is straightened out, squarely faced, and lived by each Christian, nothing will really make any sense. Altars facing the people, new catechetical methods, new pastoral approaches, the Church entering new levels of involvement in the secular world—all these will remain sterile without the personal confrontation with God.

Because the essence of all that Vatican II stands for is the conversion of every individual to the gospel of Jesus Christ, the deepest thing that the Christian can give to the secular world, that for which it is hungering most, is God.

Christians must first of all be one with Christ through a conversion that is beyond words to describe. They must be totally "with Christ," following his words, "Those who are not with me are against me." The Christian of today must be totally with Christ, and that without any rationalization or compromise! For Christ, the resurrected Christ, the Lord of history, is the one who will act through the Christian upon the world. It is by being totally one with Christ that the Christian will be totally present to the world.

Becoming totally one with Christ means undergoing that inner conversion that Vatican II demands of the Christian. All the rest— liturgy, theology, philosophy—are but secondary tools that will only fit the hand of those Christians who have thus totally surrendered to God and have decided to live the gospel without compromise. Or, to put it another way, have decided to implement in every moment of their existence the commandment of love.

Then the problem of authority, for instance, will disappear, because Christians will become Christ's team. On a team there is mutual respect, reverence, as all work for the same goal and have the same motivation. The vision of the whole is the essence of any "training" given to Christians, especially to those engaged in specific ministries in the Church. Then the study and the role of theology, anthropology, sociology, psychology, missiology will fall into place like the pieces of a jigsaw puzzle.

Until the center of that vision of the Council becomes the center of every Christian's vision, we will not have the tranquility of God's order but only the confusion of Babel. We cannot give the world anything it doesn't already have except God and God's love. But before we can give God to men, we must be one with him ourselves. This kind of "program," this kind of "approach" will be unchangeable until the Parousia. There has never been any more effective program than to live the gospel with one's life.

Should Church Conform to World?

Must the Church conform to the world and its modern ideas in order to be understood and heard? Much depends on the clarification of the word "conform." The answer is "yes" if by conform is meant change and adaptation in order to express eternal truths in a way more understandable to modern man.

The answer is "yes" if through gifted sons and daughters like Teilhard de Chardin and others the same eternal message enters our scientific world and makes a synthesis of it and God's revelation.

The answer is "yes" if conform means shedding the old symbolisms that were clear to generations past, but are utterly unclear to present generations. Such things as titles, modes of dress, cultural forms that belong to the past and that will never return.

On the other hand, the Church cannot conform to the world as understood by Christ in his parables. To this world there can be neither conformity nor can we compromise with it. On the contrary, toward this world the Church and every Christian must be prophetic. We must cry out loudly the word of God, ready even to be stoned as were all the prophets sent by the Lord.

Christ came to stir up people so that they might be aroused from their complacency, indifference, hedonism—that they might arise and follow him.

No, when it comes to any compromise with the message of the gospel, there can be no giving of ground. Christ said very clearly, he who is not with me is against me. The Christian and the whole Church must cry out loudly and uncompromisingly the glad news, even if the world considers it bad news, disturbing news, unpleasant news. Christ came to disturb the consciences of men. The people who continue his mission must also continue to disturb.

Perhaps some of the problems in this area are a matter of semantics. Many people may not understand that there is a kind of conformism which is still based on love and which never compromises. On the contrary, it stands out as Christ stood out in his time, as Truth itself. It stands out like the prophets of the Old Testament, who cried out the words of the Lord to a stiff-necked generation of Israelites who resemble very much our own generation.

A Christian is one who loves and who brings the message of love.

True love never compromises, never conforms to anything which is not the truth.

Whatever Happened to . . .?

Can one write a little meditation by simply asking a series of questions? Why not?

What happened to charity (whose other name is love) in the postconciliar Church? How will our non-Christian and our atheistic brethren come to know God if we do not love him, our neighbors and our enemies?

Whatever happened to the notion of sin? We have almost forgotten how to spell it, so little is it written or spoken about. Has it become an obsolete word, archaic? Or worse, has it become an indecent word, not to be mentioned among Christians—especially "enlightened" ones?

What has become of Mary, the Mother of God, who even the modern scripture scholars *agree* was the Mother of God? Or should Catholics forget all about this woman's fiat which brought about the Incarnation?

What of the devil, the Prince of Darkness? Perhaps he has become as Dostoyevsky described him in one of his novels, as the "man in a business suit," an ordinary guy whom you would hardly take notice of. Or has the postconciliar thinking done away with him also?

Does the Church need reforming? The answer is a resounding "yes." But how should it be reformed? According to the dictates of charity and the unchanging teachings of Love, or according to the intelligence of men who try to conform Christ's teaching to their own? Do we want to preach the gospel of Christ or our own gospel? Which shall it be?

On the answer to these questions depends the future of Christianity. Will the Church go into the catacombs? Will it become a

Church of the diaspora?* Will it be splintered into little pieces? Will it form a community of love that will show the wounds of Christ to modern doubting Thomases?

What shall it be?

Renewal Begins With Me

A strange weariness—or perhaps even more than weariness—a strange pain seems to be entering the minds and hearts of Catholics. This weariness, this pain often comes from the Catholic press, from its books and its publications. Its criticisms, of course, are necessary, for without them stagnation would set in. But criticisms that constantly aim at the magisterium and administrative arms of the Church, criticisms that are constantly negative, that highlight the weaknesses and sinfulness of the people of God (especially those in high places), such criticisms can create depression of mind and heart, a depression that by its very weight brings discouragement, weariness, sadness and pain.

Too infrequently has the Catholic press discussed the essence of the Vatican Council and the conversion it calls for. For the essence is that each individual open the windows of his own mind and heart and begin a renewal in himself!

Factually, what the Council did was to bring Christians back to the gospel, emphasizing its essence, which is love. Men must begin to love. It is impossible to prove the existence of God intellectually today to people. They must see him in our lives. The proof must be existential: The Christian must cry the gospel with his life.

If Christians would live the gospel, far-reaching political, economic and social changes would take place. Criticisms, then, should begin with oneself, and from there the whole Church, the whole people of God, would be changed. After all, it is individual human failings which impede the whole body. If each realized that the

---

*Literally, the scattering abroad of seed by the sower. Refers to the scattering of small groups of Christians in the world. Cf. Peter 1:1.

change must begin with himself, then things could be discussed joyfully, because the discussion would be rooted in the charity of Christ.

But still today, the pain of the Christian people is resulting in a slowing down of responses to the stirring of the Holy Spirit within us all. This is due to the endless stream of negative criticism that comes from the unconscious and subconscious depths of men and women who for some reason or another have long suppressed their adolescent hostilities and now suddenly feel free to express them.

We are human. We are sinners. We are creatures of God. This is a time for mutual charity. This is a time of building without destroying, for the spirit of the gospel is to deal gently and lovingly with things old and new.

We are a sick generation. We're a tired generation. We're a hungry generation—hungry for God, hungry for love. Let us help one another, humbly, prayerfully, lovingly. Let us go hand in hand toward the light and the fire which the Holy Spirit has so lavishly poured upon us through Pope John and the Council.

Let us begin with ourselves. Let us see the beam in our own eye before we look for the mote in that of our neighbor (bishops are neighbors, remember!). Only when our hearts are full of love shall we be able to speak the truth with the gentle and healing voice of Christ who is Truth. He alone is without sin. He alone can take up the cords and chase the moneylenders out of the temple!

We must not forget that to each one of us he has addressed the words, "Let him who is without sin throw the first stone." Perhaps before we criticize so negatively, we should repeat these words to ourselves.

Renewal and the Bible

Especially on the agenda of God's people should we have our priorities straight! The enemy of tranquility in the hearts of God's people is *confusion.* A confused person cannot think straight. Today we have a tremendous number of confused Christians.

The gospel clearly states that the first concern of Christians should be to seek the kingdom of God. It further states that once they have begun this search—based their whole lives on this search —everything will be given to them.

So it would seem that the first concern of Christians who are concerned with updating the Church or changing society is not to begin with the reformation of the bishops or of the priests, but with themselves. Are we really seeking the kingdom of God first? All our compromising and rationalizing are simply other forms of confusion.

How does one get confused? By allowing disorder to enter one's mind and heart. How does one get "unconfused"? By seeking first the order of the kingdom. This means taking time out from activity, from "doing good" even, and entering into the great silence of the Lord. Alone in that silence, bible in hand, slowly the terrible noise inside us will die, and the voice of God will be heard. The Book, which in Eastern spirituality is another incarnation of Christ, will speak to us in depth, and we shall clearly see which are the first items on our agenda.

Unless we do this, it is to be feared that we shall be drowned in our own inner noise of dialogues, encounters, meetings, discussions in which either all speak at once, or each speaks without listening much to the other.

Also, let us stop for a while reading what others say about the bible and let us begin in silence and solitude to read the bible ourselves. Then, when we return to our place in the world, we will have something to say. What is even more important, we will have learned how to listen. Then we might be in a position to help others see that the kingdom of God is to be sought after before all else. We may then both see ourselves and help others to see that, indeed, everything else is given to us when we do that.

Loveless Reformers

Libraries are filled with the writings of people who are trying to analyze, explain, decipher what is happening in our world. What should we do? In what direction should we turn? Catholic books and magazines are no exception. Vatican II and open windows have brought forth similar analyses. It is good for everyone, Catholics included, to examine their consciences as individuals and as a group. But it is not good to spend one's time examining the consciences of others!

It is good for the Christian to take part in peace and protest marches, but it is utterly against the gospel to turn peace marches into hate marches. Within the Catholic Church it is good to courageously face authority, whoever that authority may be. But the way to face it is a la Thomas More, who spoke the truth to kings and prelates without fear; also, he did not attempt to escape the consequences of such confrontations. And another big *also:* He did everything in charity!

Here lies the crux of our modern confusion, the almost utter confusion that at present is shaking the minds of young and old alike. How can one be a pacifist if there is no peace in one's heart? How can we heal our Black brothers, the "poor rich," the "rich poor," if we have neither the oil of compassion nor the wine of love?

We have forgotten that change, renewals, restorations never begin with "George." Nor does it continue and end in "George." It always begins with oneself. It is *I* who must feed the hungry, clothe the naked, visit the sick.

Christ said to love our neighbors. He made no exceptions. This includes even members of the "establishment" we are demonstrating against!

Perhaps because we haven't even begun to preach this gospel *with our lives* that all our protest marches, our writings—beautiful as some of them may be—fall flat and are left behind like seeds on a stony ground; they bring only more confusion into the minds of men.

Christ said that we should be like little children, for of such is the kingdom of heaven. It is a little frightening to think of his other sentence: "It would be better for him (the person who causes scandal) to be thrown into the sea with a millstone tied around his neck, than that he should lead astray a single one of these little ones." Yet, it seems that this is exactly what happens today. Many want "George to do it." Thank God for the exceptions, for they truly preach the gospel with their lives, and they are the ones who give the real answers.

Not Against Flesh and Blood

Truly, in our day and age, the mystery of iniquity and the mystery of love are confronting each other visibly, palpably, in the Church. It is truly a strange sight to behold. Perhaps it is precisely because the fire of love is among us in so visible a manner that the anger of the Prince of Darkness is drawn forth.

In every city, in every town, in every village of the world, these two mysteries confront each other, simultaneously revealing the poverty and the wealth of Christians.

Is it any wonder then that those who do not believe in God obtain more reasons for their unbelief than ever before? For nothing repels man from religion more than the hypocrisy of those who only give it lip service.

But the problem is deeper than this visible appearance. Exactly why are there Christians who refuse others the justice and love which God demands of those who would enter his kingdom of peace? Christian hearts which should be filled with love for everyone are often filled with hate. Christian hearts that should seek peace often talk and shout of war. Christian hearts which should be worshiping but one God create for themselves a thousand other gods and live by values that do not even remotely resemble the gospel of Jesus Christ.

What are the reasons for this tragic state of affairs? Is it ignorance? How can that be? Our land is dotted with schools, for example, Catholic schools and universities. What is being taught there? Has Catholic education, Catholic training, Catholic formation been so terrible that it hasn't taught the essence of our faith which is the commandment of love?

Why is there so much rationalization, so much compromise? Perhaps one answer is that God permits it to happen so that we reexamine our consciences about his commandment of love, and begin to realize that there is a mystery of iniquity at work, a Prince of Darkness. Realizing this, we will begin anew to fight him by facing squarely the great reality of Christ, by taking up the weapons of prayer and fasting with which to exorcise Satan from our personal and national lives.

I Cry to You, O Lord!

"Out of the depths I cry to you, O Lord."

If anyone were to ask why these lines come to me so often, I would answer, because I often seem to be living in the depths! What depths? Confusion? Bewilderment? Doubts? Chaos, inward and outward? No. The depths into which I am often plunged are the depths of a strange pain. It is the pain of seeing the Church rent and torn by a lack of charity!

"Out of the depths I cry to you, O Lord."

Yes, I cry to God for Catholic papers and magazines that they might print something positive about the Church, and not write only about the problems and scandals.

I cry to the Lord for priests. I ask him to give them the grace to understand who a priest is, and what the sacrament of Ordination really means. I cry that the Lord might reveal to priests the difference between their own needs and the needs of millions of people who hunger for God. I cry that priests forget their own needs and become food for those who hunger.

Daily the priest offers the Sacrifice of Calvary. His words alone can change the bread and wine into the Body and Blood of Christ. He who daily eats of Christ must realize that he too has to be "eaten up" by others. He has to forget his own needs and be concerned, consumed by the needs of others.

"Out of the depths I cry to you, O Lord."

I cry to the Lord for all religious. I ask him to give them vision, courage and strength not to leave their orders and convents, but to stay and help restore them according to the breathtaking visions of their founders and foundresses. I cry that they may forget themselves and imitate the Spendthrift of Love who called them to the orders to become spendthrifts themselves, even unto death.

"Out of the depths I cry to you, O Lord."

I cry for parents so engrossed in giving their children all the material benefits of our affluent society that they neglect to give them the only thing that matters—God. I pray that God may touch parents with the spittle of his grace, so that they may know him—may see him—and seeing him may give him to their children.

"Out of the depths I cry to you, O Lord."

I cry to the Lord for the laity, who are so many and so powerful. I ask him to cleanse our hearts of any hatred for the "other," whoever that other may be. I ask him to cleanse us especially of any hatred or fear of our black brothers and sisters, and any other minority group whose passion is daily paraded before our eyes.

I cry to the Lord for laity who write and speak without any peace in their hearts, without any charity. I pray that their words are rooted in the word of God so that they may bring peace, friendship and tranquility to the hearts of men.

I cry to the Lord for all men everywhere that they may become instruments of his peace—not seeking to *be* consoled, loved and understood, but *to* love, *to* console, *to* understand.

How foolish of me to write like this! Yet, I can't help it. I am willing to stay in these depths where the Lord has placed me. Perhaps my staying here and just crying out to him, idiotic as it may seem, will render fruitful both the depths and my pain. I hope so!

Cleaning the House of the Church

In this tremendous time of renewal after Vatican II, when the strong wind of welcomed change is blowing with full force, it is of vital importance that we do not lose sight of the true essence of our goal.

For it is easy to do so! Hundreds of questions that have been clamoring for answers are now being examined. Many old doubts are being resolved or removed.

But, on the other side of the ledger, there is always man's impatience with himself and with others. He has a desire to change and implement everything at once. In the process, new doubts, new temptations, new questions arise with startling rapidity. Such obstacles almost seem to block out the fresh, invigorating wind that came from the Holy Spirit to the Council Fathers.

We are reminded of the parable of Jesus concerning the exorcism of a certain person. A small group of devils had been exorcised. The soul was then swept and made neat and tidy. But in some way it did not keep up its vigilance. Before long it found itself again occupied, this time by an even greater hoard of devils than before.

What, then, is the goal, the true essence toward which all Christians must strive and never lose sight of? The answer is simple—and always the same—*love*. This is easily stated but, oh, how difficult of implementation unless that essence is constantly kept in mind!

For it is easy to *say*, "Love God and love your neighbor." But in order to love God as he wishes to be loved, one must do so through one's neighbor. In order to love one's neighbor one has to understand who one is, how poor one is as a creature. One has to become one of those poor of whom Christ said in the Sermon on the Mount, "Blessed are the poor in spirit, for theirs is the kingdom of God." For, indeed, it is the kingdom of God that they have to bring on earth, where it begins.

To love one's neighbor is, in a manner of speaking, to know that one cannot love by oneself, that one must love God through another. This means that one has to become empty of self. It means that one has to forget that all-important pronoun "I." In a word, it means death to all the selfishness, to all the pride in man. It means to become meek and humble as Christ was.

Yes, it means all these things and much more. One does not arrive at all this rapidly, or without effort. The journey leads to the liturgy, to the Eucharist, where alone we can find the grace and strength to become such lovers. It means for modern man a breaking up of the old and a rebuilding of the new. Both processes are painful to the soul, to the mind and heart.

It is this pain of Christ that we must enter. Yes, we must enter it in order that we may bring the essence of his teaching into the world. Strange as this might seem, we must also enter into the prayer, the vigils, and the silence of Christ. For it is there that another encounter with him really takes place. It is there too that the school of love teaches us patience, which is the martyrdom of love that we all must undergo in order to become sparks in the Spirit's wind. Only then will the Vatican Council and renewal take roots in the world, when it has taken roots in us—and when we have taken roots in Christ.

The Reform Is . . . Love

Where should renewal lead first and foremost? It should lead Christians to become a community of love. God said, "It is not good for man to be alone." God knew about communities of love. The first and eternal community of love is the Most Holy Trinity. Thus, each individual Christian must first become part of that Community of Love, part of the Trinity. He must incarnate this union into his daily life. Then he must form a community of love with everyone he meets. Other people are strangers to us, but a stranger is simply "a friend I haven't met yet." Friendship is the fruit of love.

The family must become a community of love, extend and spill over this love by forming a community with its neighbors, that is, with the rest of the world which enters into the orbit of the family's ordinary relationships. Always one must begin with oneself, must undergo a *metanoia,* a change of heart, an emptying of oneself, so that the divine light which comes from the unity with the Trinity may flow through one and draw others into that light.

This process applies to all human beings. It applies to those in the magisterium of the Church in their relationships with one another and with all those under their care. It applies to priests and to religious orders. Unless they begin with one another, loving one another, all their efforts will be in vain. They will not restructure the structures of the Church. There will be no renewal—far from it. The fruits will be chaos and confusion. For without love one cannot restructure anything in the Church whose Founder is Love.

It is because charity seems to be dying and love seems to be in some sort of deep sleep that the Church is in agony. Wounded by her own children who do not wish to pay the price of love, she is trying to be reformed by those who want to renew and reform everything except themselves.

There are many, it is true, who understand this important lesson, who really do attempt to begin with themselves and with the help of God's grace. It is these people who must take on the terrible burden of chaos and confusion which is going on in the souls of their brothers and sisters. Like Veronica they must stand by the Church in the face of lashes which seem to come directly from Satan.

The Church is in agony. The remedy: greater love, greater understanding, greater compassion, greater empathy for all who are confused, suffering, leaving the Church, tearing the seamless robe of Christ in the process. The world has become a Coliseum once again. Those who understand that true renewal begins with themselves will be handed over, as it were, to the beasts of confusion, apostasy, denials, hostilities and criticisms. They will be ground into the invisible wheat of the bread of Christ. Having eaten of the God of love, they must now be ready to be consumed themselves as holocausts and as martyrs. This invisible shedding of blood may be the seeds of both a new faith and the finding of a lost one.

Changing the Structures

In many Catholic circles there is deep unrest regarding the structure of the Church. Structure! It seems that the word cannot be used any longer without bad connotations. That some of the Church structures need to be changed, everybody agrees. But how to change them, no one knows!

Granted, structures must be changed. But the construction must be built on the folly of Christ and his cross, not on the sand of man's intellect and wisdom. That means crucifixion—but also resurrection. If we build on any other foundation, what guarantee do we have that these *new* structures will be the right ones?

Probably because I am a Russian, because I come from a different culture and background, and more probably because I have been reared on the scriptures, I see only one way of changing the structures of the Church: *Stay with them.*

Yes, stay with them. I raise my voice humbly, truthfully, without fear of consequences, even if it should mean crucifixion. I remain unmovable, like a tree standing by the living water flowing within the mystery of the Church.

During my years of experience in the Lay Apostolate, I could say that I always lived within the structures, and also experienced there crucifixion and persecution. Only God knows what effect my life had on the structures—but some of the structures *have* changed!

The question remains: to leave the structures, or to stay within them and die a thousand deaths; to leave them through despair, or to change them from within by love. It can only be with the love of Christ, the love of his own heart which he will give to us if, in the darkness of faith, we enter into the essence of the mystery of the Church. We cannot stay on the periphery of the Church's life. There we will never understand. We must enter into her tremendous, awesome mystery.

Let Us Love the Church Passionately

I am not a theologian, but I understand without understanding that we the laity have the power to send the Church into the catacombs again. For though the gates of hell will not prevail against the Church, it can become just a handful of people hiding for their lives, when it should be a brilliant light on a mountain!

We now have, in truth and in reality, an increase of charisms among the laity, and with these comes an increase in grave responsibilities. In the tremendous mystery of the Church, we sinners and vessels of clay will either show the true face of Christ to a world which hungers for him, or we will blur that image. It won't help to get too preoccupied with the human Church. There is danger of breaking the vessels of clay and allowing the world-healing ointment of love to spill on the ground instead of on the hearts of men.

The agony of the Church is in my bones these days. Long are the nights, my sleepless nights that grip me and will not let me go. I pray to the Holy Spirit for all the laity, especially the talented laity of our day, that they "trade well" with the talents God has given them.

Let us love the Church with a passionate love. Let us remember that the Church, in its sacraments and in its very being, is a mystery of love, because Christ, its head, is a mystery of love. Let us first incarnate this mystery of love in our lives, and only afterward turn our eyes to the human vessels of clay. But let us do this latter reverently, with hearts full of charity, patience and understanding. Otherwise the fog of confusion and of chaos will take hold of us and we shall be out of touch with God who is Love.

I'm sure I sound like a record with only one refrain! But if one is in agony over the Church, then perhaps there is only one refrain one can sing. After all, can the song of love be sung too much?

Young Flowers of the Spring

Priests are still leaving the Church. A deep sadness, at times, enters the souls of not only Catholics but Christians of all denominations.

Such sadness should be a passing thing. We must not forget the almost forgotten theological virtue of hope which is now buried under a million tons of negativism. There is the negativism of the young and of the old and of everyone in between!

Negation! A somber word, a heavy word. The dictionary defines it as the "refusal to consent to," "contradict." Its color tone is dark. But rising even from under the weight of negativism is hope. It rises like a crocus in the spring. It comes forth full of joy, youth, laughter, humor, with a "yes" to being. It consents to accept life as it comes from the hands of God. It has faith, not blind faith but intelligent faith, realistic faith, a faith that understands. It is a faith based on the grace of Baptism, and it has its being and its joy in the immense mystery of love.

Little by little we see young men entering seminaries. Young girls are seeking religious life. They are a new breed, with few sentimental illusions. Theirs is no weak pietism. They are young men and women who know where they are going, and why.

"Yes, I know where I am going," said a young man in a discussion group. "I am going into the seminary because I want to be a priest. I don't want to destroy, I want to build. My father is a stonemason. I helped him with his work. Stones are heavy. But when you know how to carry them and how to lay them, you finish with a beautiful house. I think that, like St. Francis, we are called today to repair the Church of Christ. So I am going to be one of those stones, and let God be the stonemason."

A young girl said: "Yes, I know that this order only has 20 nuns left. Well, I will be No. 21, with God's help. I am going in with my eyes open, my heart full of love for those nuns who must have suffered much. I enter with the faith and hope that I will make a good religious."

This trickle may be small, unimportant, hardly even worth writing about. But, then, few people write about wild flowers when they are just popping their white, blue and pink heads out of the snow. But these young people are the proof that hope is with us. Where hope is, where faith and love are, there God is. Alleluia!

The Thawing Wind of the Spirit

In sometimes obvious, but in often more quiet ways, slowly the Spirit is working his ways on modern man. Youth is seeking after new and old ways of prayer. They are turning toward the building of communities and communes. There is little talk anymore about the "death of God." Many talk about the Lord of History, about his role in our world, about penance, fasting and prayer.

Yes, a gentle breeze is blowing through our land once again. Young and old are being filled with peace. Instead of paper flowers, or even natural flowers, men are giving one another the joy of the Lord.

Many, tired of criticisms and negative approaches to life and to the churches, are taking more and more positive attitudes toward all of these. Catholic theologians are rarely read by youth and their elders, but the bible, at the moment, seems to be the most read book of all (it always has been!). Yes, to those who have eyes to see and ears to hear, there is an underground swell, but it is quiet, and very gentle and, strangely enough, it is even distinct from the "underground church."

Here and there one hears news of young people entering religious orders again, especially the contemplative orders. Here and there young people are attempting to found little groups which resemble religious orders. The gentle breeze is becoming a wind—here and there. Let us pray that soon it will fall in tongues of flame upon all Christians, whoever they are, so that someday each one of us will show the face of Christ to the other.

Quietly, without fanfare and without publicity, the Spirit of the Lord is truly alive again in the hearts of men.

Into the Arms of Hope

Let us be full of hope, for this is the era of the Spirit! We have passed through confusing times. Vatican II, one of the first signs of the coming of the Spirit in our times, shook us all up, as powerful winds are wont to do! They were powerful winds, leaving behind them a seeming havoc. Mighty trees fell, which no one knew were hollow! As they fell they tore up a lot of underbrush that had begun to grow over the paths of the Lord.

Yes, let us be full of hope, notwithstanding the fact that the wind of the Spirit confused many, upset old, established ways and customs —customs that really should have changed a long time ago. But now we can begin to assess what has happened and realize that it was so very simple and beautiful, and that only God could have brought it about.

What happened was that the Holy Spirit, the advocate of the

poor who has always been with us, has made himself known again! As on the first Pentecost, he has shaken everyone up with his winds of change. He reawakened in us truths which we thought were self-evident but which obviously we had not incarnated into our daily lives. All this gave the impression of being impelled not into the light of the Holy Spirit, but into some strange, upsetting and terrifying darkness.

But now we are beginning to see that, though shaken up, we truly have been thrown into the arms of hope—wondrous, soul-healing, joyous hope. So let us be full of hope! This is the time of rejoicing, the time of thanking God for the gift of the Spirit, eternally renewed. Let us thank him for the faith that makes hope grow by leaps and bounds.

Yes, this is the time to be full of hope, because whatever darkness has come upon us, it is now passing. The people of God are turning to prayer. When man turns to God in prayer, then God gives him the key to his heart and to the hearts of his brothers. With this key we indeed can bring forth faith, hope and love to all men.

Let us be full of hope! For this is the time of the Spirit.

Alleluia!

Chapter 3

Trinity, Sobornost, Community

The Community of the Trinity

The word "community" is on everybody's lips these days. Again and again the question of how to form a community is discussed by theologians, philosophers, religious communities of men and women—in fact, by the laity too, young and old alike.

It seems to be a sort of magic word that came from somewhere, gleaming like a freshly minted coin. But no one mentions the fact that "community" is a reality as old as the earth, as old as the universe, and older. It is a reality that belongs to eternity.

The Eternal Community is the Trinity. It has existed eternally, having no beginning and no end. The Community of the Trinity is simply the Community of Love: God the Father loving God the Son, and this love bringing forth the Holy Spirit.

In order to form a community, man must make contact with the Trinity first. Then and only then can he make a community with his fellowmen.

How does he make this contact? No one can blueprint this for him, but there are basically two elements involved: prayer and man.

Man can find God through man because Christ's incarnation brought all humanity into himself and he entered all of humanity.

Prayer brings man directly into contact with the Trinity, but prayer also returns him inevitably to his brothers. Again, because of the Incarnation, man has been readmitted to the Community of the Trinity, to the Community of Love.

But no community can be established among men if men decide that they do not need the Trinity or Jesus Christ, or think that they can make their own God. Then chaos reigns instead of community.

The secret of becoming a community is a total involvement in the other, and a total emptying of oneself so that each can say, "I live now, not I, but Christ lives in me." Then the Christian community has come into existence. Then, like the Holy Spirit who truly formed it, it is a fire burning in our midst; from this fire sparks kindle the earth.

Prayer and love . . . love and prayer . . . children of faith and sisters of hope . . . these are the ingredients that are needed to form this community. Nothing else will do!

The Trinity and Sobornost

A new word makes its appearance these days in Catholic magazines. It is a word very familiar to the people who follow the Byzantine rites of the Church or, perhaps more accurately, to those in the Eastern spirituality traditions. It is a simple word: *sobornost.*

Sobor means generally a cathedral, usually the one where the bishop of the diocese is in residence, and where, on all major occasions, his priests and people gather around him to offer the Eucharist and to praise God.

Sobrania means a gathering, in a somewhat similar sense to the the word liturgy which is basically a gathering of people to perform some kind of communal work.

Sobornost, though having *sobrania* (gathering) as a root, has a much different connotation. It has some kinship with the English word "collegiality" but it still is as far removed from this word as the earth is from the moon! It has a much more profound meaning for the people of the East. It is not a word that should be used flippantly. This is a special hazard today when so many foreign words are entering our language. No. It is a very holy word, an awesome word. The word lies in great depths, and its incarnation into the lives of people is something like a spring that wells up from the very heart of the most Holy Trinity.

Perhaps this reality of the most Holy Trinity is the best context in which to approach the true meaning of *sobornost*. For in the trinitarian life there is a complete and total unanimity of heart and mind (if one can express it that way). And *sobornost* begins in the heart of a people whose prayer life is spent before the Trinity and is a reflection of the Father, Son and Holy Spirit.

When the people of God truly become bound, as all Christians should be, by the will of the Father, into a community, they take on the obedience of the Son, and they rely for total unity of mind and heart on the Holy Spirit, the Advocate, whom the Father sent to remind us of all that the Son has taught.

Sobornost, therefore, is a unity of mind, heart and soul among Christians who truly desire to preach the gospel with their lives, clothe it with their own flesh. *Sobornost* is the manifestation of the unity Christ asked us to live and reflect when he said, "that they may all be one, even as thou, Father, in me and I in Thee. . . ."

Sobornost should create among the faithful neither dependence on authority nor independence, nor even interdependence. It calls for life on much higher spiritual planes and levels. It calls for a oneness in the Body of Christ so totally at one with him, and hence with the Father and the Holy Spirit, as to become in truth a trinitarian body, as Christ must have been during his life on earth.

Sobornost is achieved by intense and constant prayer. The members of the community, of either religious or laity who function within the ideal of *sobornost,* must become lovers and servants of one another. The function of authority in such a community—bishops, priests, superiors, fathers, mothers—would be that of suffering servants of Yahweh, people of the towel and the water, for all Christians must wash the feet of all men even as Christ washed the feet of his apostles.

Yes, authority would be the servant of all, willingly crucified for the needs and the salvation of all. Authority within the spiritual understanding of *sobornost* would be in love with God and man. The members of the community functioning within the ideal of *sobornost* would be lovers and servants of one another. All together would be constantly alerted and aware of one thing and one thing only: that they are not many but *one* in the Lord.

Sobornost is a mystery given by God to men as the gospel solution to the deep spiritual problems that might confront families, religious communities, communities of laity and, perhaps, someday, the community of Christian nations.

No, *sobornost* is not a word to be used lightly. Its mystery can only be approached and achieved through prayer.

Liturgy and Sobornost

As the renewal of the Church proceeds, there are moments when I become confused, and it takes time and prayer to become unconfused! Coming as I do from Russia (the Eastern accent of the Church being part of my very being, my thinking and my faith), I felt there was something I was missing, something I wasn't quite understanding, especially in the liturgical renewal.

I understood perfectly (and rejoiced in it immensely) when the vernacular was introduced into the liturgy. The altar facing the people also was beautiful and meaningful. Guitars, new songs—all of these I saw quite clearly had to be part of the renewal. I accepted them joyfully. Concelebration was literally a delight to my heart. Communion under both species was nothing new to me. In the Russian Church and in the Eastern rites, this way of receiving Holy Communion has existed from time immemorial. I was glad to see that now also in the West the laity were being permitted this experience.

But, as time went on, this liturgical renewal, this constant experimentation, began to worry and confuse me. It didn't seem to be bringing forth the expected results. It didn't seem to be forming a "community of love" of those who were offering the sacrifice and of those who participated in it—those who had received the Lord together.

I listened to the comments of learned theologians, of eminent liturgists, and the rank-and-file religious. I listened to the avant-garde groups, the ones who are "in" on all the latest things. I listened to those who were not "in." I got more and more confused.

Everybody seemed to think that the nonessentials were important. Many confused nonessentials with essentials. It seemed to me that they were confused too. People attending the most avant-garde Masses would leave the Church without talking to one another, without welcoming the stranger in their midst. It was as if they had enjoyed themselves immensely, felt a oneness with the others as the Mass was going on but, afterward, in some strange way, reverted back again to being private individuals.

It took me a long time to realize what I was up against. I had been brought up with a very simple idea which was and is part of my faith: that a Christian is never alone, simply because he is a Christian.

Do I recite the rosary alone or with others? Am I engaged in some vocal prayers? Am I making the Way of the Cross by myself? Do I enter total solitude? Do I read the word of God and contemplate the Lord in a chapel or in my room? It doesn't matter, really. At all times and always the whole Christian community, the whole world of humanity, is with me, present to me.

The ideal that needs to be realized again is *sobornost,* the community that forms one complete, indivisible whole to which you always belong, from which you can never be separated, precisely because you are mysteriously *one with all the others* who form that *sobornost.*

This concept of oneness with humanity—this belief that we're all bound, through Christ, with the bonds of love—is a living incarnated, existential part of Eastern Christianity. The West evidently developed (due to historical reasons with which I am not all that familiar) a pronounced individualism. The people of the North American continent in particular seem to value very much their sense of individuality.

In recent years the concept of the Mystical Body of Christ had begun to penetrate into people's thinking. Now the phrase "people of God" is being used more. But to a Russian like myself, the word "body" is still more meaningful and understandable than that of "people of God." "Body" and *sobornost* go better together.

Sobornost finds its roots, its essence, its very reason for being in the Holy Sacrifice of the Mass. It's Christ who brings about oneness, and all of us together are united in his love for us, our love for him and our love for one another.

Therefore, in the Eastern and Russian mind, it isn't too important if it's a private Mass (although we do not celebrate private Masses in the Russian Church very often), a Mass with or without music, Communion under one or both species—these do not make the community of love. These are helpful but secondary elements. We believe in, feel and live out our oneness in every form of prayer we know. It is inconceivable, in a sense, for a Russian to pray alone. Whatever form his prayer takes, the whole body of Christ, the people of God, are present within him. He just cannot "pray alone."

I watched the renewal with great joy and gladness. I welcomed what, to my mind, were tools to bring about a real community of love to the people of God and to the West. The West seemed to be estranged from the idea. I admit that I became fearful that the blessed renewal of Vatican II would stop at nonessentials, instead of plunging the modern Christian into the very heart of the love of God.

The essence of the Mass is the consecration. Those of us who have been at those secret Masses in concentration camps which were both said and attended at the price of one's life know what this means. Often these Masses consisted only of the consecration of the bread and wine—bread and wine stolen from the Nazis or Communists. There were no songs, no guitars. There was nothing else.

There was nothing to mar the essence, nothing to distract from it. Those Masses are unforgettable to those who experienced them. There was oneness with Christians everywhere, with all of humanity; it was a living reality. The community of love that is formed among prisoners and those who are persecuted is beyond human words to express.

Don't misunderstand me. I am for any means (used with the proper approval) which will help bring Christians to the realization that the basis of the formation of a community of love is the reception of Christ at the most holy sacrifice of the Eucharist. From this essential gift of God to us—the gift of himself in the sacrifice and sacrament—the community of love is formed. Anything that brings us to this realization is good.

We must remember that because we are Christians we are never alone before God. We are an integral part of one another. What binds us together is love and only love. Love is a Person, love is God. The experimentation now going on in the West is an attempt to bring this concept of a community of love from heads into hearts. I pray to the Lord that we never confuse the essence of things with what is nonessential.

Community and Change of Heart

On all sides, among all nations, peoples of all races, men of all creeds, everywhere people are seeking answers not only to peaceful coexistence but to all their deepest needs of friendship and peace. Everywhere people search for deeper communication between one another.

People are coming together in small and large groups, forming communes and communities of all shapes and sizes. In a few months, a year or two, some of them break up and dissolve. Young people move in pilgrimages across wide expanses of continents in search of understanding, of communication in depth, of the answer that could bring unity and peace.

But the search will be in vain unless each one of us—each one of us who forms part of a larger community of family, parish, town, city, nation—begins with a personal change of heart. For there can be no community, no peace, without a deep inner change of heart. A community is based on love, a love that is all-embracing, that accepts, with grave humility, the other, no matter who he is—black, red, yellow, white, sick, healthy, ugly, beautiful, old, young.

To accept the "other" as he is, without trying to manipulate him, is the beginning of the establishment of a family, a village, a nation. Without this basis of the love which flowers into full acceptance, no peace can come to the individual or to a nation.

How does one change one's heart? It is truly impossible to do it by oneself, but it is possible through prayer. Truly, the time of prayer is at hand. It is the only thing left for us now since all the other ways have failed.

Technology is bringing us a million changes a minute, one might say. Without a change of heart we will not be able to use the benefits of technology but only abuse them to the detriment of the common good—abuse them even unto the destruction of one another.

Let us pray to the Holy Spirit then. Let us do it now, that he may help us change our hearts. For on this change of our hearts depends the immediate future of mankind.

Foundations of Christian Community

The way some people talk about community today, it seems the whole world is interested in banding together, perhaps just to be together. At times, one is afraid to be alone. Life may become a threat, and loneliness is surely one of the maladies of our times. But communities and communes are not made in a day, nor can they be set up by an order or directive from the "top" somewhere. They cannot be formed merely by a desire to "be together," to "be less lonely." Such motives cannot make a group of people into a community.

A community is an organic reality. It must spring from one heart. There must be a cause, a reason which makes a group band together in the first place. And the reason must be greater than oneself, greater even than the good of the collective. Usually the reason is spiritual. For the Spirit alone can hold people together; he alone can insure permanency.

Communities can be found throughout the whole history of mankind. Even today, in India and in other Far Eastern countries, such communities exist. Always they are based and held together by deep spiritual convictions and by the worship of someone greater than oneself. Communities that were not founded on such a supernatural base flourished for a while, then disappeared soon after their foundation.

The communities that have the love of God as their bond are the ones that endure. The people in such communities realize that they come together, not for any ordinary reason (for example, to "return to the land"), but to incarnate in society the law of love.

This means that such people were drawn, even before coming together, to a life of love, and hence to the service of God and mankind. They come ready for discipline, a personal discipline which is absolutely necessary for living together with a group of other people.

Actually, communities of this sort are made up of very "foolish" people, for the wisdom of God is the foolishness of men. Let us review, for a moment, what it means to be a member of a Christian community. We speak here predominantly of a Christian community, not in the sense of a city, village, or even parish, but of smaller groups who come to live together out of love for God and man.

First and foremost, members of this community must love God with a totality that is absolute, always tending in faith toward that absolute throughout their lives. Entry into such a community means to become a pilgrim of the Absolute. He who becomes a pilgrim of the Absolute must be absolutely dedicated to this ideal.

Secondly, it means loving your neighbor as yourself. Here is the catch: Before you can become a dedicated member of any community, you must love yourself. Love yourself by accepting yourself as you are, by stopping the manipulation of others. It means a constant effort toward achieving poverty, purity of heart and embracing the ideals of St. Francis, ". . . not seeking to be consoled but to console, not to be loved, but to love." This is what is meant, in part, by loving one-self. There is more, but the rest will come slowly from the Holy Spirit.

When one begins to love oneself, one can begin loving one's neighbor. Even more than incarnating the words of St. Francis, we must incarnate the words of God himself.

God said, "By this shall all men know that you are my disciples, if you have love one for another." Obviously, this is impossible! For who of us can love with the heart of God? We cannot. But we can enter into the immense travail of emptying our hearts of everything that impedes the coming of the Lord, so that in time we can say with St. Paul, "I live now, not I, but Christ lives in me."

As this happens, the community begins to be cemented together by love. Now it grows strong, having grown organically, and having recognized that its growth is contingent on God's law of love.

But it must go further. Each member must love those who hate him or her. Here the foolishness of the cross bites deeply. For above all they must love any member of their community who appears to be hurtful to them, who appears to "hate" them.

This, like the emptying, the *kenosis,* will require prayer. The members of any community of the type we are treating here must be people of deep prayer. In fact, constant prayer. Without prayer the law of the love of God cannot be incarnated.

We must go one step further: Such a community must really enter Love, the Absolute God. For God is the Absolute. God is Love. Members of the community must plunge into him. St. John of the Cross says, "I plunge into the abyss to catch my prey." Each must be prepared to fulfill Christ's last commandment of love: "Greater love has no man than he lay down his life for his friend."

Those people who are drawn to this totality of the ideal of plunging into the Absolute should be the ones to form the Christian community. They will be the ones who will be the icons of Christ, that is, the ones who will reflect Christ, make him available to those who no longer believe in mere words—those who are seeking for the Incarnation in other men.

Yes, a Christian community can be based only on God and his incredible, immense, wondrous law of love. It is this love which is the need of the times. Nothing else will do.

Community Is Loving One Another

I was asked a while ago to speak to a group of religious concerning the "Formation of a Community of Love." What I had to say was simple, pertaining to what I consider is the real essence of things. That essence is summed up in St. Paul's beautiful hymn to charity in the 13th chapter of I Corinthians.

For our community at Madonna House St. Paul's description of charity is the essence, the base, the cornerstone of the formation of a community of love, and we feel that nothing matters except to enter into his words and incarnate them in our lives. We know that even before St. Paul spoke those words, Christ had spoken very clearly about love: "By this shall all men know that you are my disciples, that you love one another as I have loved you."

No matter how long or how many times I meditate on that gospel passage, I am overawed by it. God seems to ask the impossible. We who are called his disciples, his followers, are asked to love one another *with his heart!* How can an ordinary person love with the heart of God?

Nevertheless, this kind of love is the essence, the cornerstone, the foundation, *the answer* to all the questioning, confusion, turmoil and unrest which are presently shaking us bruised reeds. First, foremost, and last, before we talk about techniques, sensitivity courses, interpersonal relationships and all the rest, we must ask ourselves the following question: Have we begun to love the people in the community God has placed us? It may be a family, a lay apostolic community, a religious community, the parish, a village, a neighborhood. Have we begun to love the people with whom we live?

Unless we start with this conviction that only by the love which Christ can give us shall we be recognized as his disciples, all else will be chaff in the wind!

How does this idea apply directly to religious communities? It seems to me that somewhere along the line this essence was, not lost sight of exactly, but perhaps rationalized a little. I realize that the structure of religious communities, especially the teaching ones, gives intense attention to the needed competencies demanded by the institutions they serve. Religious go through a period of novitiate, a juniorate, then they may be sent on to complete their academic work. These studies take up a tremendous amount of time, and often continue for years.

This, it seems to me, places a tremendous burden on individuals. Separate rooms are needed for study and the correction and preparation of papers, etc. All this can very easily lead to some kind of "island" existence.

I suggest that perhaps no one should go out to study until at least the roots of that community of love are solidly planted in each heart. Then the individuals can go forth to study or teach, because then, wherever they go, they will etch the face of their Beloved on blackboards and in books. Without difficulty, they will form communities of love with their pupils, fellow students and with all people. Perhaps then the time of the juniorate should be extended, so that the young sisters could learn really to love one another and become a community of love, living together in a simple dormitory-style life, so suitable to a true *kenosis,* as well as to true love for one another.

How can one recognize if the roots of love have taken hold? When the individual is concerned, not about himself or herself, but about everyone else.

Yes, young religious are hungry for knowledge. So are all men. But greater than the hunger for knowledge is the hunger for love. We Christians are called to show forth Love, who is a Person, in our lives. If we want to live in any religious community—any community for that matter—we must begin by loving one another.

Until we do this, we shall not be able to show the face of Christ to anyone. We may be able to share our academic knowledge, our various competencies, but the kingdom of God will not have the first place in our lives. If it does not, then, as Jesus said, nothing else will be given to us. We shall be empty-handed.

Of course, many religious these days are trying to devise ways and means of loving. Some think that by going into the ghetto they will both find and be able to give that love. Some religious are living in small groups in apartments; others are becoming lone apostles in some special mission or situation. Many are the techniques being used to achieve these communities of love.

But Paul's letter still rings in my ears. I would paraphrase it something like this: "If you go into the depths of the ghetto and have no love . . . if you break up into smaller communities and live in apartments . . . if you expose yourself to death by joining the revolutionaries in Latin America . . . if you do all these things, but without love, you are still like tinkling brass and clanging cymbals."

It seems to me that my theme song, whenever I am asked to speak anywhere, to priests, nuns, or laity, is the same: that we must love one another as Christ loved us, and this in whatever community he has placed us. We must love one another with Christ's own heart, with a total surrender to God in the other. To form such a community of love means accepting the cross, carrying it, and being crucified on it. Only then can we live in the resurrected Christ.

Wherever there is love there is pain, sometimes a terrible pain that tears us apart—but only so that God can put us back together again.

Such is the essence of forming a community, and we must begin with this essence or we will fail. Since we are human and cannot accomplish this of ourselves, we must make contact with God through whom, by whom, and in whom alone we can achieve this miracle of love. Prayer, therefore, is also of the essence—the prayer of the Eucharist, and the constant prayer of the heart. The prayer of silence too. All such prayer will lead us unerringly to the essence.

Training to Love

Not only Christians, but the world in general, especially the world of youth—all are desperately trying to get in touch with God in one way or another. All kinds of university courses are being set up to teach catechetics, scripture and theology.

Many priests, nuns and lay people often ask me what kind of program, what kind of course, what kind of training I consider is needed in our days. They ask how we train people in our apostolate at Madonna House.

Strangely enough, I am hesitant. The answers do not seem to come easily to me. I was brought up in the Russian tradition, which emphasizes normal, human, family relationships. The "gurus" were parents or teachers or someone in charge of the very young.

I don't know if these people could be called "charismatic" or not; they simply had the tradition of Christianity at work in them: a love of the Trinity, a deep understanding of the role of the Holy Spirit in the life of man, a living understanding of the scriptures and participation in the "liturgia" as the Russians called the Mass.

Real training and formation came from someone who lived what God preaches, or tried to, and that someone was a person who had made "contact with God" through prayer and action.

No wonder Thomas Merton found his way to the East in order to discover how the guru was able to reach down and get into the depths of a disciple. It is difficult for the Western mind to comprehend the guru-disciple relationship. It exists in Russia too, for Russia is part of the East, and a very important part. Russia, in many ways, has absorbed much of the Eastern wisdom. It has also brought to the West a more direct continuity with the early Christians, and indeed with Christ himself. The guru-disciple relationship was the way the Master himself taught.

Yes, I have to hesitate when questions of training are posed to me. I hesitate even more when people ask about contacting God. "How do I meet Christ?" people ask.

I have found no shortcuts in meeting Christ. I have found him in the humble day-to-day routine of human existence. Perhaps it began with my mother and my father, but especially my mother, who seemed to connect, so easily, so simply, the daily life of a little girl as she grew up, with God. Yes, this was my tradition: All things are related to God, and one can find God in them.

Perhaps this is why I really find it so difficult to outline, in any logical, intellectual way, my answer to those who ask me what training should be. I feel like shouting, like crying out, "Why do you ask me, it is all so clear. The training we must give is the training Christ gave his apostles, and which the apostles gave the early Christians. The training that made them capable of going to the arenas of the pagan world; the training that eventually made slave and master one in the same household."

I think modern youth understands my hesitation. They too seek the guru-disciple relationship. Their search for God is increasing. They are truly hastening to find the Lord.

It is obvious too that the Holy Spirit is indeed "training" us today. The Seat of Wisdom is making us wise without too many "courses," just to show us how one can meet God in the Mass, in the word of God, in the following of Christ from Nazareth to Calvary. It is to be folded in the wings of the Crimson Dove, as the Russians call the Holy Spirit. These are the answers I would give to questions of "training"!

The Role of Christians Today

The role of Christians especially will be to establish communities of love and to show to others the mutual love of the members, one for another. In this way they will present the face of the living God, the resurrected Christ. He will so powerfully dwell in such communities that, far from being dead, he will be touched and seen in those who call themselves his followers.

Thus will the Thomases of today, those who believe that he is simply dead and not resurrected, be able to see him, be able to put their fingers in his wounds and to see the radiance of his countenance.

Yes, the role of the modern Christian is changing. This does not mean that he will abandon the corporal works of mercy. The poor will always remain with us. But the accent of the modern times will be to show that Christ is alive, that the Spirit is with us as he never was before, in a continual Pentecost. Where the Son is, there the Father is also. This can only be shown by the growth of love among us so that all the neopagans, all the atheists of today can say again—will be compelled to say—"See how those Christians love one another."

This is the witnessing that we, the people of God, must do today. We can only do it by praying for an increase in faith, in courage, and love. This is the hour of love and of loving. God is love. We must bring him into the marketplace. The time is now.

Chapter 4 / *Love*

The Revolution of Love

Christians are called to become icons of Christ, to reflect him. But we are called to even more than that. *Ikon* is the Greek word for "image of God." We are called to incarnate him in our lives, to clothe our lives with him, so that men can see him in us, touch him in us, recognize him in us.

When we don't live the gospel without compromise, or try to, we are skeletons. People do not care to deal with skeletons. The gospel can be summed up by saying that it is the tremendous, tender, compassionate, gentle, extraordinary, explosive, revolutionary law of Christ's love.

He calls each one of us who calls himself a Christian. He calls us directly. There is no compromise in his call: "Whoever is not with me is against me. . . . If you love me, keep my commandments." We can find umpteen quotations in the gospel that will vividly bring forth to our minds and hearts how simply and how insistently he calls us to be like him, and to accept his law of love without compromise.

His call is revolutionary, there is no denying it. If we Christians implemented it, it would change the world in a few months. The gospel is radical, and Christ indeed is the *radix,* the root from which spring all things. His commandments mean risk, great risk. They imply a lack of that security to which most men cling so tightly.

The security to which most people cling is a mere illusion. We are not secure walking the streets of a large modern city. In planes we never know if we'll stay up or not. Wars flare up in almost every part of the world. So where is that security that everybody is supposed to value so dearly? God doesn't give us this material security. He offers instead faith, a faith which begins, in a sense, when reason ends.

God offers us risk, danger and a strange insecurity that leads to perfect security. His security begins when we start loving God with our whole heart, our whole mind, our whole soul and our neighbor as ourselves. I speak of this so often but it is the only message that can never be overstressed. We must clothe the skeletons of our lives with the flesh of his love, or we shall perish.

For this kind of loving we have the Holy Spirit in us. With his help we shall be able to love our neighbor. With him we shall have the courage to *risk* loving the neighbor. It is a tremendous risk, because we must also love our enemies. Once we have entered into Christ's law of love, we have the power and the grace, the charisms, to change enemies into friends and beloved neighbors. To love one's neighbor is the ultimate risk, for it may even mean death for my brother's sake if need be.

All this sounds very idealistic and perhaps quite unobtainable. Christ assures us it *is* attainable. It is through those strange little steps day after day that one slowly accepts the other as he or she is, begins to love totally, tenderly, compassionately. Once this has begun, the involvement becomes deeper and deeper and deeper.

As this involvement of love between brothers grows and deepens, we enter into a revolution. A revolution in which there is a violence directed only against oneself. There is much to be overcome, so terribly much, before we can say with St. Paul, "I live now, not I, but

Christ lives in me." This kind of warfare truly brings about a revolution in the individual and in the community of mankind. The revolution of Christ brings about a whole new set of values.

My brothers and sisters in Christ, I implore you before it is too late, clothe the skeletons of your flesh with the love of Christ. If we do, we can lead the world and humanity out of the terrible and hellish depths to which it has sunk. There is so little time.

The Gospel Without Compromise

Are Christians becoming a smaller group in this immense secular world, a group that doesn't matter very much, a group that is merely tolerated? It all depends on one's point of view. Sociologists, theologians and other specialists may think so. But ordinary lay apostles working in the heat of the day, in the unchartered frontiers of the Spirit, may not agree with these conclusions.

Daily, hourly, we deal with people whose hunger for God is unlimited, who will go to any lengths, march to any location, in order to find God.

Perhaps it is a bit farfetched to say that young rebels are pilgrims of the Absolute, that those who take drugs are searching for God. But we know that this is so because we meet them constantly and listen endlessly to their hunger for things spiritual, for a meaning in life; we see in the hurricane of their confusion the eye of the hurricane.

Listening day in and day out to the modern music of the young, we clearly hear the psalmist crying, "Out of the depths I cry to you, O Lord. Hear the voice of my supplication."

The longer we live, the more we realize that there is literally a massive search for God taking place—the God of the Christians. People are searching for the carpenter of Nazareth, the poor itinerant preacher, the God-man who died, literally, for love of us.

The problem does not lie in the fact that we seem to be living in a diaspora situation. The problem is that we Christians do not understand that the world is always hungry *for the reality that is Christ.*

Guitar Masses are interesting, but they soon pale. Change is exciting, but man cannot live on change alone. Change must be a road leading to the essence.

What is the essence? Christians who love one another and who form communities of love. Humanity today is the Doubting Thomas who wasn't there when Christ appeared for the first time after his resurrection. Humanity today is a man who must touch the wounds of Christ in order to believe, to be converted. Then he will come to the Lord in thousands, perhaps in millions.

The only way to show these wounds of Christ to others is to *live the gospel without compromise*. Does that mean that we must turn our lives upside down? Does it mean a complete change of values? Does it mean the breaking up, the demolition of our comfortable way of life? Quite simply, yes, it does.

When we who call ourselves Christians show forth the gospel in our lives, the searchers for God, these pilgrims of the Absolute, will see him, will touch him, and they will believe.

It is time that we showed all men the face of the resurrected Christ in whom we and all creation have our being. It's time that we cease to bemoan our miseries and begin to love one another, to form communities of love to which all others can come—communities where people can touch, see and feel the wounds of Christ. Yes, we who work in the heat of the day, in the front lines of the spiritual warfare, know that this is the true and only answer for a world which seeks so desperately for meaning in life.

The Gospel With Compromise

It seems that it is time for all of us Christians to face God and to tell him, "Yes, Lord, we are with you, for where else can we go?" or to say, "No, Lord, your sayings are too hard, and we shall not follow you any longer."

A sense of deep sadness comes over me when I think of how Christians sit on the fence. What is the matter with us? Have we forgotten that we are followers of a crucified Christ? Have we forgotten that he was just the son of a carpenter, himself a tradesman, a strange itinerant preacher who crisscrossed the tiny country of Palestine, preaching his gospel to the poor? Have we forgotten that from the moment he began preaching he walked in the shadow of death? Have we forgotten that following him means to take the greatest risk that man can take? Have we forgotten that following him means living dangerously?

It seems that we have spent centuries trying to eliminate the risk and the danger of his call. It seems that we have cushioned the risk and practically eliminated any and all danger by drawing up a set of moral rules that give us security instead of holy insecurity; rules that lull our conscience to sleep instead of making it wide awake and ready to undertake the risks of being a Christian.

Christ said that if we are not with him we are against him. How do we measure up to this saying of his? Are we really *with* him? Are we ready to give up father, mother, sister and brother, in the sense he means it, that following him demands? Are we ready to lay our lives on the line of his law of love with its fantastic dimensions of dispossession and surrender? Do we truly love one another, beginning with ourselves?

I wonder how long we can sit on the fence of compromise. God is not mocked!

We have to begin to love one another in the fullest sense of Christ's teaching. But to do so we must pray. It is only through prayer that one can follow Christ to Golgotha and up onto the other side of his cross, and to become free through this ascension. The immense problems of war, of social injustice, of the thousand and one ills that beset our world, these can be solved only if we begin to love one another. When man begins to see love, respect and reverence Christ in the eyes of another, then he will change, and society will change also.

Christians must openly declare their allegiance to Christ, or their nonallegiance to him. The story of the disciples who had to choose is repeating itself today among us. "Who do *you* say that I am?"

Peter, for the other apostles, openly declared himself for Jesus. On another occasion, Christ's words were too harsh, and other disciples admitted it and left him. It is time we did likewise and stopped fooling around. If ever there was a time when humanity needed followers of Christ and fewer fence-sitters, that time is now.

Love Is the Answer

Our world is certainly experiencing the storms of national and international turmoil. How tragic and pitiful it is that man cannot experience that inner peace which is his heritage from Christ. Especially is this true of Western men, most of whom are baptized and grafted onto the body of Christ.

How simple and how timely the gospel is. In it lie the answers to our problems. The gospel is like a light shining in the darkness. Why is it then that we who are Christians refuse to even try the clear answers of the gospel? Why do we wish to constantly compromise, water down and eliminate from the gospel whatever is too hard for us? Why settle for such a pale reflection of his strong words and loving teachings?

We seem to have tried everything that our intelligence and genius can come up with. But so far, if we are to be judged by the fruits of the tree, we certainly have not succeeded. Nor are we leaving our children a better world to live in. On the contrary, we are leaving them a more chaotic world than even the one we inherited.

Why then do we not try the way of love, the way of the gospel? Why do we not apply the gospel without compromise to our personal, national and international life?

Love could bridge the gap between Christians and Jews; after all, we Christians are spiritual Semites and the Old Testament was the forerunner of the New. The love of the Father became incarnate for us, and he was a son of Abraham.

Love could bridge the gap between Jews, Catholics and Protestants. We all believe in one God, the God of love. Why then could we not live by the law of his love? What is stopping us?

Why can't we believe that only Love, who is God, can walk upon the stormy waters of our times and quiet them? Love is the only answer, and it has to start in the mind and heart of every human being. Only then will it be effective.

Leadership in love must come from those who profess to be followers of Christ, of the God of Abraham, of Yahweh. Yes, let us cry the gospel with our lives and the whole world will enter into its springtime, and the storms will be hushed, and peace will reign among us.

Do You Realize God Loves You?

The greatest tragedy of our world is that men do not know, really know, that God loves them. Some believe it in a shadowy sort of way. If they were to really think about it they would soon realize that their belief in God's love for them is very remote and abstract.

Because of this lack of realization of God's love for them, men do not know how to love God back. Often they don't even try, because it all seems so very difficult, and so very, very remote.

For too many people, the Christian faith is a series of dogmas and tenets to be believed, commandments and precepts to be observed and obeyed in a negative fashion. Of course Christians should believe in the dogmas of their faith; of course they must observe the commandments. But Christians must also realize, with a joy that can scarcely be expressed, that the Christian faith, in its essence, is a love affair between God and man.

Not just a *simple* love affair: It is a *passionate* love affair. God so loved man that he created him in his image. God so loved man that he became man himself, died on a cross, was raised from the dead by the Father, ascended into heaven—and all this in order to bring man back to himself, to that heaven which he had lost through his own fault.

Yes, of course, the Christian has dogmas he must believe in order to be a Christian, but all those dogmas concern love which is the essence. God is love. Where love is, God is. Dogmas and tenets of the Christian faith without love are dead letters, not even worth spelling out.

Yes, of course, the Christian must observe the commandments, the commandments given on Mt. Sinai to Moses. These same commandments were confirmed by Christ, luminously, forcefully, gently and vividly. But they must not be obeyed negatively, out of fear or compulsion. The essence of both Testaments, New and Old, the essence of all the commandments, is still love, always love, the immense love of God!

These commandments simply spell out the love affair which God asks man to engage in. The commandments simply tell man to love his Lord and God, the Tremendous Lover, and to love his neighbor as himself.

The greatest tragedy of our age is that men do not realize, or perhaps do not want to realize, that God loved them first, and that their whole peace and happiness consist in loving him back.

It is time we awoke from our long sleep, we Christians. It is time we shed our fears of God, or what is worse, our indifference toward him. Then we shall know true peace, true joy. The answers to our international and national problems will become clear in proportion as we love.

The Tremendous Lover

How strange that modern Christians seem to miss the greatest point of their faith! To so many, God is the "Man with the big stick." The great commandment to love God with all one's heart has been turned into a yardstick of implacable justice: "Toe the line or else you'll go to hell!"

The love affair between God and man seems never to have touched the hearts of many religious people. They do not seem to realize that the fulfillment of religion is a return of God's immense love for us. They do not see that the tremendous glad news is that God first loved us.

Because of this lack of awareness, because of their fearful attitude toward God, the lives of many Christians are full of fears. For these they seek many remedies everywhere except where the remedy can alone be found—in God. If only they began to love him back passionately, totally, completely, as Christians should, realizing that every word he has said, every commandment he has given, is a commandment of love. Every commandment leads to true freedom, happiness, peace and joy—the very things that everyone is seeking so desperately everywhere.

It is quite clear that the task of every Christian is to be the leaven of the world by bringing this glorious, wondrous, joyful truth to the hearts of men. Everyone, every baptized person should go about the world proclaiming this one truth: *God loved us first. Let us love him back. Let us learn to obey his commandments and implement his counsels so well that the world and the hearts of men will know, at long last, the peace of the Lord, and will understand and incarnate in their lives the immense truth that perfect love casts out fears, that it sets men's hearts free and brings joy and gladness into the drabbest existence.*

To understand that the Christian religion is a love affair between man and God, to begin to love God back passionately as he loved us, this will, if implemented and incarnated in the lives of Christians, also bring peace to our hapless world, and a solution to the seemingly unsolvable problems of our marketplaces.

Let us begin now. Let us arise and meet the Tremendous Lover before it is too late.

Heartbeats and Love Songs

The liturgy is slowly doing away with many private devotions. Yet, it will never do away with the devotion to the Sacred Heart because the Sacred Heart of Jesus is the essence of the liturgy expressed in simple and human terms.

For man, the heart has always been a symbol of love. The liturgy was born out of love, Love who is a Person, who is God. It is inextricably interwoven with that symbol of love, the Sacred Heart of Jesus.

Long ago and far away an ordinary man called John laid his head on the breast of Christ and listened to the heartbeats of the Lord. Who can venture to guess what that man felt as he heard the beat of that mighty heart? None of us can ever be in his place, but all of us could hear, if we would but listen, the heartbeats of God, the song of love he sings to us whom he has loved so much.

If we love him back we can learn from everything, from every creature, the answering song of love that should dwell in our hearts daily. If we stop to listen to the liturgy of nature, to its rhythm, to its songs of obedience to the laws of the Creator, we could hear and learn how to sing our love song back to the God of love.

If we listened to the songs of the city, to the noises that sometimes irritate us, we would realize that even they, in their own way, praise God. The songs of the machines would praise God too if we kept them where they belong—as our servants and not our masters. Yes, even the machines could teach us how to return the love of the Sacred Heart. If we meditated deeply on the Eucharist and on the themes of the Liturgy of the Hours, we would distinctly hear the loving, powerful, immense heartbeats of God. We would hear more; we would hear that heart speaking to us.

If we meditated on the most holy sacrament of the Eucharist we would not only hear his heartbeats, we would hear our hearts beating in unison with his, we would be united with our Lord and our God.

So let us enter the great silence of our own souls. Let us pray there humbly, lovingly, plunging into the riches of the Sacred Heart. Then we shall know God in a way that no book can tell us or teach us. Then we will love him so passionately, so tremendously, so utterly and completely, that it will become simple for us to be the kind of Christians we must be. We will not have to *say* very much. We will only have to walk upright, crying the gospel with our lives, reflecting our Lover in our faces.

The world needs the Sacred Heart. The world needs human hearts united to the Sacred Heart. Without love the world is very dark. Let us arise and resurrect the world by bringing love to it and it to God.

Love Is Someone

Many people today are trying to define both what love is and who God is. The two can never be separated. It is because men today separate God and love that we have confusion, turmoil, doubts and so many chaotic situations, not only in the Catholic Church but in all Christian churches.

From the pulpits, God is preached and love is preached as perhaps never before, and yet the essence of love seems to escape those who preach and listen. Perhaps this is too strong an indictment. The Lord said, "By their fruits you shall know them." What are the fruits of the average churchgoing Christian? Oh, I'm sure there are many wonderful fruits, but too often they remain hidden, buried somewhere. Perhaps it's good that this be so, and yet the Lord also said that we should not hide our lights under a bushel basket.

Christians go to church and receive the Body and Blood of Christ, but often forget the words of St. Paul: "Whoever eats the bread or drinks the cup of the Lord in an unworthy manner will be guilty of profaning the body and blood of the Lord. Let a man examine himself, and so eat of the bread and drink of the cup. For anyone who eats and drinks without discerning the body eats and drinks judgment upon himself."

How can we come to understand what love is, who God is? It is plain that we cannot understand if we desecrate his Body and Blood in each other. Until we fully understand that God is love, that love is not a state, not an emotion, but a Person, we shall never understand either love or God.

It would be better to stop calling ourselves Christians—followers of Christ who is Love—than to scandalize our brothers and sisters by going through the motions of being Christians, rendering lip service only.

First, *Love the Lord Your God*

From much of the current religious literature, one definite notion seems to be taking hold of Catholics and other Christians: that we must seek Christ in our brother. The notion seems to imply that the personal approach to Christ in the sacraments and other so-called "old-fashioned ways" is obsolete. The concentration of the Christian seems to be on justice, on abolishing poverty, on social work, on interpersonal relationships, encounters and so on. More and more, one reads that the best way to encounter Christ is in and through another human being.

Here is where the question becomes acute: "How can I find Christ in my brother if I do not know him personally first?" It seems to me that I cannot recognize him in others if I do not first meet him personally.

What do I mean by this "personal meeting"? Perhaps I mean the very essence of the *mysterium* of our faith. He gave us two commandments: to love God, and to love our neighbor. In that order! But to love someone I must know him. To know him I must meet him. Then I will recognize him in others.

How do I get to know him, so that I can love him and continue to love him in my brothers, and to love my brothers because I love him? I know him because I was baptized into his death and resurrection, and because he knew me first. I know him in the Breaking of the Bread. I know him in the sacrament of repentance (which the Russians call the "kiss of Christ") when I kneel in sorrow in confession. I know him through the Holy Spirit who came to me in his immense power at Confirmation, and who abides with me always.

I know him in prayer, prayer of all kinds, but especially in the prayer of silence. In the inner silence of my own heart he comes with his own intense silence. There he breaks open my heart, quiets the noise, and inspires me to say, "Speak, Lord, for your servant is listening."

Yes, I could learn much *about* him through study, books and other tools of the mind. But there is a difference between knowing *about* God and *knowing* God. Only those to whom he reveals himself *know* him. This brings us back again to prayer and the sacraments.

It is through these that we make a vital contact with Jesus Christ, the Father, and the Holy Spirit. It is through these that we get to *know* God. Only then, it seems to me, can we go forth to others, to our brothers, to all humanity, and there recognize him in men.

This seems to me to be of the essence. All the rest of what I read seems to be peripheral, like a moth flying around a flame. How can we love men if we do not love God first? How can we love God first, if we do not seek to know him, to meet him as a Person? How can we possibly recognize him in men if we have never met him?

If our love of God, the fruit of which is our love for men, is not present, why do we not call ourselves what we are—humanitarians—instead of Christians? "How can I find Christ in my brother if I do not know him personally—if I do not love *him* first?" I have given my answer. If anybody has another, I'd be glad to hear it.

Real Love Isn't Easy

With all the current talk about "love-ins" and discussions about "love" in general, love still remains a mystery to modern man, especially modern youth. Perhaps it remains a mystery because they try to dissect it as if it were a butterfly which can be caught and analyzed chemically and classified under its proper species. Love eludes such intellectual approaches because love is not a thing, love is not a state. Love is a Person. Love is God.

It may help us if we reread what Jesus Christ has said about love. It might help if we meditated on his words and made them our own, made them both the way and the goal of our lives. For he told us first to love God with all our hearts, with all our being, and then to love our neighbor as ourselves, which implies that we must first learn to love ourselves well. He also said that "by this shall all men know that you are my disciples, that you love one another as I have loved you." Finally, he said, "Love your enemies."

Yes, he defined all the ways of loving. He not only defined them, he lived them. He was Love incarnate, and he showed us in truth that "greater love has no man than that he lay down his life for his friends." Love has no limits.

Perhaps that is why there is so much talk about love, so much experimenting, and so much disappointment too with what we imagine love to be. Because deep down in our hearts we know that his way of loving is the way of the cross, that it is painful, and that it demands an emptying of ourselves. Without his loving us, none of us could love the way he wants us to.

Christian love is allowing Christ to love with our own hearts. But in order to do this we must make room within ourselves to allow him to grow to his full stature. That means emptying ourselves from our self-centeredness, our egoism, from the desire to have all our needs fulfilled. It means that we must get busy filling the needs of others.

True, all this spells pain to us moderns who take sleeping pills and tranquilizers by the ton to alleviate the slightest anxiety and pain. But if we arise and follow this road of love, we shall know joy beyond the telling. Incredible as it may seem, if we follow that road of love which Christ etched out for us, we will solve most of our modern problems. Charity, whose other name is love, will then prevail among all Christians, and the problems of religious orders, priests, families and even nations may solve themselves in an atmosphere of peace and joy.

It seems as if the world needs fools—fools for Christ! Fools for God's sake! For it is such fools that have changed the face of the earth.

To Love or Be Loved—That Is the Question

Why is it that we do not understand the word "love"? Why is it that it is always used with connotations of starry-eyed lovers, roses and sentimental music so prevalent on radio and TV?

Yes, love can be equated with marital love for, like all real loves, marital love has its source in Love who is a Person, who is God. The scriptures make this comparison in a profound and beautiful way. There is the Song of Songs which describes the love between God and his people in terms of the love of man and woman. Yet, in our modern world, even marital love suffers desecration by gooey sentimentality and tragic unrealism.

Love is a Person. Love is God. Where love is, God is. Where God is, love is. All vocations are vocations to love. A vocation to marriage or a vocation to the religious life, to the priesthood or to the single life, all are vocations to love.

But the word is so misunderstood. Because it is, infinite tragedy stalks the world. Marriages are broken up every day, smashed, because men and women have never understood what loving means, who love *is*.

The result of a recent poll taken among both sexes by a Catholic lecturer in a Catholic college revealed one rather strange and frightening reply. The question: "Why do you want to get married?" The overwhelming response: "To be loved."

It was an informal sort of survey, but its results brought fear into the heart of the lecturer. The real answer should have been: to love.

If a young person enters into the holy vocation of matrimony "to be loved," and both partners have the same idea, then who is going to do the loving? The problem is profound indeed. Perhaps psychiatrists, psychologists, doctors, priests and theologians should come together to find out why our modern youth understands so little about the vocation to love which is the vocation of every Christian.

Psychiatrists say that "to take and not to give is the sign of emotional immaturity." It is normal for a child between the ages of one and four. But real emotional maturity is equated with an attitude of giving and not of merely taking all the time.

Long before this world knew anything about psychiatry, the Lord of Hosts, the Son of God Almighty made man, the Great Physician gave us our Christian vocation. He gave us the unfailing recipe for Christian joy and Christian happiness. He simply said, "Love the

Lord your God with your whole heart and with your whole mind and with your whole soul, and love your neighbor as yourself."

Simple words, yes, but of infinite depth; words that describe love exactly. This definition of love does not connote sentimental love songs. Rather, it shows love as something strong and beautiful. Love does not ask to be loved in return but it serves, knowing that it is a reflection of him who is Love, who came to serve and not to be served.

True happiness is found by forgetting the word "I" and remembering the words "he," "she" and "they." The time is ripe to teach our youth the true meaning of that, at one and the same time, little and immense word—love.

The Theology of Self-love

In these fantastic days (which often seem more like dark nights than days) we go about talking of love, especially love of our neighbor. It is true, many of us have finally decided that to know Christ is to truly arrive at love of the neighbor, and in this meeting alone we can find our Lord and God.

There is truth, of course, in this statement, or is it only a half-truth? Christ gave us two commandments, to love God with our whole heart, mind and soul, and to love our neighbor as ourselves.

There is a lot of talk about the neighbor, but few mention the fact that before this we must love *ourselves,* "your neighbor *as yourself."*

What about this loving of ourselves? It doesn't take a vast sociological survey to tell us that very few people accept and love themselves in the proper way, love themselves so as to be able to properly love God and their neighbor.

I don't know if there should be a "theology of loving oneself." It is doubtful because so many theologies exist already. *That* we leave to the psychiatrists and psychologists. In the meantime, we keep very busy with our involvement in the ghettos, our M.A. and Ph.D. programs, all of which we do presumably in order to love and serve our neighbor better.

Could it be that in much of this we are running away from ourselves and don't want to meet ourselves? Are we busy running away from the Trinity within us who waits to teach us how to love *ourselves,* so that in truth our hearts may be open to God and man in a godlike way?

We don't take time to stand still and listen to the voice of God within ourselves. We are afraid of being alone with ourselves. We have forgotten that man is never alone. Man may leave God out of his life, but God does not leave out man.

No Love, No God?

Where love is God is. But can God be present where there is no love? We talk much about love. The word is in our songs, discussed on TV programs, lauded in sermons!

But how much love is present in the hearts of men so that God can really enter them and be at home? It is becoming more and more difficult to listen to the word "love" be bandied about so constantly and be so little incarnated in the daily, nitty-gritty living of human beings.

The heat of the day gets more intense. The noonday devils are indeed roaring lions all around and about us. Humanity walks in contradictions and paradoxes that tear its soul apart!

All around the world millions of human beings are starving and dying. Why is it that massive relief from all countries, from everywhere, doesn't pour in from the hands of all those who talk so learnedly, so constantly, so theologically, so beautifully about love, about God?

Where love is, God is. Is he absent, then, from nations that kill one another, waging hopeless wars that lead nowhere except to the death of thousands? "The agony of Christ continues unto the end of the world," wrote Pascal, the French philosopher. It continues in his Mystical Body.

Whenever there is no love, Christ is rejected and killed again on a thousand Golgothas that are going on almost all over the globe with most of its people not even noticing.

In every large city of the Western world the poor are still stretching out their hands for crumbs which fall from the rich man's table. There is no love from the rich to the poor. A few crumbs fall, but never enough to make the poor feel loved. Doesn't anyone see that in each of the poor it is Christ who begs?

When, oh, when, shall we who call ourselves Christians begin in truth to be Christ-like, and to love as he commanded us! "By this shall all men know that you are my disciples, if you love one another."

Showing the Wounds of Love

Today, across a confused world, man seeks Christ! He seeks the reality of Christ, or, to put it another way, he seeks the *real Christ,* the Christ of the gospels, the one he has read about but cannot seem to find.

In this seeking men ask one another, "How do you find Christ? Where is he? Where can I find him?" Who, then, is this Christ that they seek? Why does he seem to be so illusive, so unreal, so difficult to meet? It seems to me that the answer to these questions is exceedingly simple: We meet Christ in a real Christian.

What a strange and seemingly simplistic answer! Yet, it is the true answer, and I don't think there is another. Man has to be *shown.* The time of mere talking is over.

After his resurrection, Christ showed his disciples his wounds and they believed. These wounds were visible signs of Christ's love for them and for all of us. No one needed to say anything, least of all Christ. Thomas the Doubter was the only one who spoke.

Today, it seems to me, we must likewise show the wounds of Christ to men, for then they will believe. This is what men are seeking today: someone who will show them the wounds of Christ so that they may touch him and be reassured!

But we must go further. Christ prepared breakfast on the beach for his friends. We, too, by our service, must *show* how much we love our brethren, all those who are seeking the Lord.

But even all this—to show the wounds, to prepare meals—is not enough. One must open one's heart with a lance by taking that lance in one's own hands. We must accept all human beings as they are, without wanting to change or to manipulate them. It is a benediction and a joy in itself that they come to us.

Men will not know God unless we, their neighbors, their brethren, show Christ to them in the tremendous love that Christ had for them. This is the acceptable time, so that people may once again say what was said of the early Christians, "See how these Christians love one another"—and us!

Yes, we must open the doors of our hearts. We must open the doors of our homes. We must accept people as they are. We must serve them, and we must show them the wounds of our love. Love is always wounded because love and pain are inseparable. Even as a young girl barely falling in love is worried about her boyfriend traveling on a wet road to Chicago, so in the love of people for each other, pain is interwoven. There is no love without pain.

But how do we acquire these wounds that we must show? Where do we get the strength to cook a supper for someone when we ourselves are already exhausted by the day's toil? How do we get the strength to open the doors of our hearts which we so readily want to close against the noise of our incredibly noisy world?

How, how, how? The answer comes irresistibly. We cannot hide from it or ignore it or make it disappear. The answer is always the same: prayer.

Let's face it. We cannot love the way we ought to. God alone can love in us that way. So we must empty our hearts of all the things that are not of God.

The Lord said we must love our enemies. Until we do we cannot show Christ to other men. We must go further: We must lay down our lives for our brethren. By emptying ourselves, according to his commandment of love, and with his grace, we can allow God to love in us.

No, words are not enough. But a loving glance, a wound, a

breakfast cooked for a friend, a welcome through an open door into an open heart, these will do it. It is only then, when my brother has been filled with my supper, when he has beheld my wounds of love for him, when he has experienced a totality of acceptance, only then will he be open to the glad news!

People of the Towel and the Water

"What are we to do about Christianity?" Perhaps that is the wrong question. Perhaps we should ask ourselves, are we Christians? For some it is an excruciating question, for others tragic, for still others it is superficial. For some people it isn't a question at all.

To be a Christian means to live in such a faith, in such a commitment to Christ, that it will revolutionize, turn upside down not only our lives but the lives of others.

To be a Christian means to incarnate, actualize, literally implement the teachings of the gospel. It means preaching the gospel with one's life. This alone would be a revolution, a spiritual, intellectual, political revolution!

True, certain signs of an awakening are becoming visible. The charismatic movement is sweeping the world. The hearts of men have been opened to the Holy Spirit. The churches are beginning to show more concern for the poor, the so-called useless ones, the retarded, the halt, the lame and the blind. It is also true that the churches were always on the side of such people, but the climate has changed somewhat. Today Christians are coming to the poor more as servants than as benefactors.

Yet, something is still missing. A vibrant, passionate totality of commitment seems to be missing. A cry out of the very depths of our souls for an increase of faith that would transcend all limits of time and space is missing. What is missing is the vision that deals with every event of life in the light of Christ's teaching. What is missing is a discernment which can distinguish between security which depends on man and the security of faith which is the heritage of the Christian.

It is true, prayer is flourishing. Praised be the Lord! But if we touch God with one hand, so to speak, we must touch humanity immediately with the other, or God shall walk away. For he has incarnated himself in order that he might give birth in our hearts to the law of love for one another.

The law of love demands that we become people of the towel and the water, that like Christ we wash the feet of our neighbor. This simply means that we wash the feet of one another when we implement the gospel. That and that alone is the true revolution that will change the face of the earth. It is late in the day. What does it mean to be a Christian? It means to revolutionize the world the way Christ wanted it to be revolutionized. When shall we begin?

Taking Courses in Love!

Sensitivity! Interpersonal relationships! Fulfillment! Involvement! Encounter! Commitment! Doing "my thing"! This is the vocabulary of today, at least part of it. The majority of these words are used by Catholics in their discussions and conferences. What is even more tragic is that people are even *taking courses* in sensitivity, interpersonal relationships, in order to achieve fulfillment and to understand commitment and involvement. It is as if people want to take a course in *love!*

But there are no courses in love, because Love is a Person. Love is God himself and one cannot take a course in God, no matter how theologically instructed one may be. One is like a baby learning to say "mama" and "dada" when one speaks of God.

One can take a million courses *about* God who is Love. But that doesn't mean one will know God or know Love, for the Lord does not reveal himself to those who seek him with their intellect alone. He reveals himself to those who seek him with reverence, on their knees.

Sensitivity, interpersonal relationships, involvement, dedication, since they are all children of Love, will never be learned in courses. Only in simply loving! Also, there is a Book from which these things can be learned, provided that one reads that Book on one's knees, provided one prays and meditates about what one has read!

If one commits oneself totally to Christ, then everyone will be sensitive to the other, and interpersonal relations will not have to be taught for money which could go to the poor. Strange as it may sound, *if we not only cry the gospel with our lives, but also live it to the hilt while proclaiming it, we will be fulfilled to the brim, and overflowing with fulfillment.* Most certainly, we shall be involved with our neighbors whoever they might be. To love is to serve, to be involved.

It is amazing how far a human being can deviate from a goal he is seeking! True, the path that leads to what most Christians seek is very narrow and steep. It involves, above all, *faith.* It is hard, though joyous. It does not permit tranquilizers and euphoriants. It demands the ability and the maturity to look reality in the face.

Perhaps it is because we do not want to do these simple things that we take so many courses which lead us nowhere, except on a merry-go-round without any music, turning us 'round and 'round and 'round!

Let's Stop and Notice One Another

Man today is crying out for recognition. He wants to be a person among other persons. He wants to be noticed, not in any ostentatious way, not because he might have or not have money, but just because he is a human being, a person.

Each man is on a pilgrimage, seeking to encounter others like himself who have the same needs. The greatest need of all is the need to be loved. But we pass by one another without noticing, without stopping, without the slightest sign of recognition. This is why modern man daily comes closer and closer to despair, and why he frantically continues to search for the one who will love him.

His search is for God. But God isn't easily found if he isn't reflected in the eyes of men. It is time that Christians began to take notice of each person they meet. Each person is a brother or sister in Christ. Each person must be "recognized." Each person must be given a token of friendship and love, be it only a smile, a nod of the head. Sometimes it may require the total availability of one person to another if they are to fulfill a particular person's hunger for God. Such love and recognition must always be given with deep reverence, irrespective of the "status" of the person encountered.

Reverence, understanding and hospitality of the heart—these are the immediate, intense needs of men today. Are we Christians going to wake up and act as Christians, incarnating the law of love into our daily lives in real depth? Or are we going to compromise and allow men to continue to plunge into their dark nights looking for someone to say to them: "My brother, I am here. Come. I have water and a towel. Sit down. Let me wash your tired feet that have pilgrimaged for so long. Yes, I am here. I know you. I revere you. I recognize you as my brother. I love you."

These meetings are the true crossroads of time and history. When we meet there, will we act as Christians or not?

Hospitality of the Heart

What the world needs most today is the hospitality of the heart. True, some of the young "hippie-types" are hospitable to one another. But the hospitality that is needed is much more profound. The hospitality of the heart means accepting all others as they are, allowing them to make themselves at home in one's heart.

To be at home in another person's heart means touching love, the love of a brother and sister in Christ. Touching the love of another means realizing that God loves us. For it is through the other —our neighbor, our brother—that we can begin to understand the love of God.

This is especially necessary in our strange technological loneliness that has separated us so thoroughly not only from our neighbors, but from our fathers, mothers, grandparents, in short, from our relations. Yes, our technological age has begotten a terrible loneliness! We must begin to give the hospitality of the heart. In other words, we must open ourselves to a sharing of friendship that is rooted in the very heart of Christ whom we call our friend.

We have to shed our "stiff upper lips." We have to be open to the other, share with the other, express our love for the other. This can only be done if we open the doors of our hearts. Let us do that now, before the doors of our hearts are frozen shut by some new technological achievement!

We Need Violent Christians

For a time there was much talk about nonviolence. Much was written about it. Young people of the campus world and people in all walks of life talked about it. Certainly the examples of Gandhi and Martin Luther King—one a Hindu and the other a Christian—served to focus the interest of the world on this deeply spiritual way of bringing peace to a world filled with hate and violence.

Someone wrote recently that "It is hate that makes the world go 'round." How can one remain nonviolent in the face of hatred, hostility, bodily attacks? How can one stay at home, passive, noncommitted, noninvolved when confronted with attitudes that endanger both life and sanity?

Yet, it is true, in the midst of all this violence, the hunger for peace grows, the number grows of those who elect to embrace nonviolence as a means of eradicating violence. Perhaps men are beginning to understand that when we cease to burn with love the world will then truly turn cold.

To put it another way, true nonviolence has its roots in love, a love that really believes that it must lay down its very life for the other. The nonviolent must be motivated by a dream, and there must be nothing wishy-washy about that dream. It must be rooted in faith—faith in a cause, faith in a Person, faith in God.

Without faith, nonviolence is impossible. There will come a moment of choice, a moment of standing at the crossroads of decision. A decision that may well entail life or death. Strange as this may seem, to be nonviolent, to make such decisions, to be ready to lay down

one's life both for the other and for one's beliefs, demands *violence.*
Yes, violence to oneself. For heaven is taken by violence. True
nonviolence must begin with violence to oneself. The nonviolent of
whom Christ spoke are the pure of heart who will see God. They are
the meek who will inherit the earth.

What does violence to oneself mean? It means to be humble, to
be poor, to be meek, to be pure of heart, to be empty of self, of selfish
motives. It means to have a dream that is dreamt in God.

It is this novitiate of preparation and cleansing that includes
prayer and fasting, as was the practice of Gandhi and King. Only
through this kind of novitiate is the ability, the grace, the charism of
nonviolence achieved.

Yes, one must become violent in regard to oneself with a violence
that is gentle and persistent and which comes from the Holy Spirit. It
urges one to cleanse oneself from everything except love, and to create
within a climate that will give birth to an unconquerable courage. It is
this burning with love which alone will enable us to preach nonviolence and to be nonviolent!

Like One Another As I Have Liked You

Is it possible to love all humanity? Does God want us to love all
humanity? Collectively? Individually? Should Christians, men and
women religious, for example, break up into smaller groups? It seems,
they say, that one can love better in smaller groups!

Aren't we confusing words today as well as their meaning?
When we talk about small groups, large groups, loving better, etc., do
we mean *liking* or *loving?*

Obviously, Christ didn't mean liking, for he told us to love our
enemies whom we obviously don't like. His commandment also obviously means to love *all men,* because he told us to love one another as
he loved us. He loved all men. We too are called to love all men,
those we like, dislike, even those who wish us positive evil.

"Liking" is an emotion, while "loving" is a Person. God is love,
and where he is, there is love. But if we allow "liking," the emotion,

to guide us in the choice of whom we are going to love, then we end up loving no one, except perhaps ourselves, and that in the *wrong* way.

If a few people come together in a small group because in some natural way they "like" each other, then they will merely be fulfilling the needs of one another. There will be no need to turn to Christ. There will be no need to fulfill the one need for which we have been created—our union with him.

Yes, for our wholeness, for our mental health, each man must have a friend. But what is friendship? It is never exclusive. It is two people, hand in hand as it were, going to God—but never forming a closed circuit and simply feeding on each other. They always have one hand free to hold anyone who comes into that friendship.

Even marriage is subject to this rule. Husbands and wives will have happy marriages if they are also friends! But their circle will increase very quickly, and they will have to have two hands open to clasp the hands of their children. The family—husband, wife and children—will have to have, at both ends, open hands to grasp their neighbors'. Eventually, then, all will form a community.

Is it possible to love all humanity? Indeed it is, and the sooner we begin, the sooner the global village will become a nice place to live in.

The Christian's Unique Role

The paradox of truth, of God, of Christ, marches on. Today, the teachings of Christ, as never before, are penetrating the whole world. In fact, "Caesar" is applying them on an immense scale. Christians and non-Christians are caught up in the luminous fruits of Christ's teaching, in an ever-growing realization of the dignity of man. There is a growing effort at the just distribution of goods and at least the beginnings of a hunger among men for unity. On the other hand, there is a proclamation that "God is dead"!

Thus, our time in history is at one and the same time a rejection of God and an acceptance of his teaching. The word "love" is heard all over the world, but he, the source of all love, Love itself, is being rejected, reckoned as dead, and, at times, even buried in effigy!

There was an age of faith once. At that time there was no questioning of God's existence. There was a beginning of the effort to apply his teachings to men. Social justice, the equality of men, their dignity—all these were "on the books" so to speak. But these things were not yet incarnated, whereas faith was universal in the Christian world.

Today, it sometimes seems that just the opposite is happening. Faith is on the wane, and yet the teaching of Christ is incarnating itself ever deeper. "Caesar," the governments of the world, have taken over the corporal works of mercy, the works of love, the fruits of God's teaching; these used to be the firstfruits of faith in the age of faith.

Education is passing from the hands of clerics and lay Christians into the hands of Caesar. Thus, our economic and political ideals, which are deeply rooted in the teachings of Christ, are being disseminated across the world. The paradox of the truth, the paradox of the gospel, continues. We accept the teachings of the God-man, whereas we crucify him again. If we do not crucify him, we simply declare him dead!

What, then, is the role of the people of God, the people who realize that by their Baptism they are meant to preach the gospel with their lives? We are all apostles of the Lord. What is our role today in the midst of this paradox?

It seems that our role is to show that God—the Father, Son and Holy Spirit—is more alive today than ever, and that the resurrected Christ is in our midst, and that we live in him. This can be done only by showing to others the face of God. We must establish communities of love. First, each Christian must make contact, a primary contact, with the eternal community of love which is the Trinity. Having made this contact, he will be able to make a community of love with everyone he meets. This means first of all his primary community—family, religious community—and then any other community into which this love will lead him.

Essence and Heart of Love

"Greater love than this no man has that he lay down his life for his friend."

Jesus spoke these words. But what is more, he incarnated them, dying for us a tortured and painful death.

Everyone speaks of love, everyone writes about it. Everyone asks, what is love? The answer can be found in the scriptures as to what love is.

"If I speak with the tongues of men and of angels but have no love, I am a noisy gong or a clanging cymbal. And if I have the gift of prophecy, and know all mysteries and all knowledge; and if I have all faith so as to remove mountains, but have no love, I am nothing. And if I give away everything that I have and if I deliver my body to the flames, but have no love, I gain nothing. Love is patient, is kind; love is not envious or boastful; it is not arrogant or rude. Love does not insist on having its own way; it is not ill-humored, it does not brood; it does not rejoice at wrong but rejoices in the truth.

"Love bears all things, believes all things, hopes all things, endures all things. Love never fails. Prophecy will end, and tongues will cease, and knowledge will pass away. For our knowledge is partial, and we prophesy in part. But when what is perfect comes, what is imperfect shall have an end.

"When I was a child, I spoke as a child, I felt as a child, I reasoned as a child. But when I became a man I gave up childish ways. Now we see in a mirror, obscurely; then we will see face to face. Now I know in part; then I shall know fully, even as I have been fully known. Now faith, hope, and love remain, these three, but the greatest of these is love" (I Cor 13).

Can anyone add anything to this? Let us stop the "childish and ill-humored" ways. Let us stop brooding. Let us begin to bear many of the things we will have to bear through our ever-changing civilization. Let us continue to hope, never losing hope. Let us endure all things, for love never fails. Then and only then will we be able to call ourselves Christians and celebrate the Eucharistic paschal mystery which is the essence of our faith and the greatest fruit of love.

Chapter 5 / *Poverty*

The Poorest of the Poor

I am almost frightened to write anything more on poverty. Poverty is discussed in the *New York Times* and in the *Christian Science Monitor,* not to mention the slick and the not-so-slick magazines. Even *Fortune* had something to say about poverty, contrary to its title and its usual writing trends!

But for the moment, I am not interested in what these papers and magazines talk about, world poverty. I am interested in the poverty that makes men rich. I am interested in the poverty that makes man free. I am interested in the poverty which, if it were combined with a true love, would change the physical poverty of man into decent, normal living conditions. World wars would stop. Air and water would be cleared of pollution. The poverty I am interested in is the poverty of the gospel.

Frightened as I am to discuss it, I have reached a point at which I have to speak about it, for this word burns like a fire in my soul. I believe that evangelical poverty is still often discussed on a somewhat superficial level. As Christians, we haven't dug deep enough into what poverty is all about.

The gospel requires what no political mandate would ever demand from its adherents. On a world scale, only an economy based on need and not on profit has any chance of succeeding. This requires *sacrifices* and *renunciations*. The *essential principle is to be found in independence with regard to all possessions.*

I know what it means to be poor, destitute, cold, hungry and alone. I've spent 36 years of my life in the rural and city slums of Harlem and Canada. But did I have the right to go to those tenements, to the poor, to seek Christ in those hovels and alleyways *before I found him in the manger of my own heart?*

Christ seeks himself in every heart. Will he find himself in my heart? Why should I arise and go to the slums? I should know that it is a useless journey, that he will not be there, unless he is in my heart. Neither will going to the poor with an empty heart do either them or me any good. Even if I kneel before them, it will be a lie. I may adore him in their hearts, but such adoration will be sterile and empty, because he does not dwell in mine.

It seems to me as if everybody in the Catholic world is suddenly rushing to the poor. Everyone is boarding a bus, train, or plane to go and do something for the poor and the downtrodden. These "invisible ones" have been with us for a long time. Now they become the newly discovered land to which all must go and *do* something.

No one seems to want to begin at the beginning! The beginning, of course, is ourselves, each one of us. *We are the unknown land.*

Christ said, "Love your neighbor *as yourself.*" Who is this self that God wants us to love first, before we try to love anyone else? Am I not the poorest of all? Would I take a bus, train, or plane to discover my own utter poverty, my own need of God?

It seems to me that we have misunderstood the essence of Vatican II. The pentecostal fire has not really touched us deeply, has not seared our hearts and minds with its cleansing fire, has not given us the gift of tongues, one of which would make us intelligible to ourselves.

The crisis of today is not exactly the poor, though they are part of it. *The crisis of today is man himself.* This exodus, this flight from oneself into feverish activity, is often a flight, an escape from meeting oneself. Living in the slums and offering our manifold competencies to the poor is not the answer—or I should say is not *the* answer, not the *first* answer. Others also—communists, humanitarians of all kinds —have many of the same competencies we have, and often in greater depth.

What then is it that we have to bring to the poor? First, it seems to me, the realization that *we are the poorest of the poor.* Secondly, a realization that unless we truly love ourselves, we cannot even begin to love our neighbors. Should we not begin with these things?

The crisis of today is the crisis of faith. It isn't the liturgy, it isn't social justice, it isn't the poor. It is faith. Without faith we cannot love ourselves, cannot see the image of God in our own hearts. The crib of our own hearts is empty of God. If we do not see him in ourselves, we will not be able to see him in others.

Only then can the Christ in us meet the Christ in the other. Then and only then can we go to the poor to feed them both the bread they need to live, and the bread of justice, their restored dignity as human beings. But above all, we must give them the bread and wine of Christ's body, his living words of truth. In a word, we must bring them Christ for whom they hunger without even knowing it.

Yes, before we kneel before the Christ in hovels and broken-down tenement buildings, we must be able to kneel before the Christ in our hearts. Is he there? This is *the* question, and it concerns the very essence of poverty. Are we merely seeking to run away from facing our own poverty, the crisis of faith within ourselves, and escape into the lulling, consoling, emotionally satisfying world of the poor?

Poverty of the Heart

Strange, that when we think of poverty, we think of little children with distended stomachs, having no clothes, food or shelter. It's true, this is poverty, but it is only the face, only one aspect of poverty. We will never know what poverty really is until we stop being avaricious, gluttonous and preoccupied with ourselves.

Poverty is the face of Jesus Christ, because no one was poorer than he. The Second Person of the Most Holy Trinity became man and in that process he became utterly poor. Can you imagine what it must have meant to Jesus Christ to be a man when he was God? We cannot penetrate too far into what such experiences might have been. For him to become like us (in everything except sin) was true poverty.

St. Francis fell in love with Lady Poverty. To him, with his Italian imagination, she was a beautiful lady. No wonder Christ entered into the mystery of poverty. Christ made "Lady Poverty" his own. This is a mystery so delicate, so incredible, that one can only stand before it and wonder if we will ever experience the joy of espousing Lady Poverty as Christ and St. Francis did.

But for us, poverty has other dimensions. Poverty is also to give up what we might call manipulation. People rationalize and say that if we hand ourselves completely over to another, we cease to be ourselves. The truth is that this handing over of ourselves to Christ is total poverty.

We like to manipulate people. We like to treat people in such a way so that they will treat us the way we want them to. We use masks all the time. We are afraid of rejection. But really poor people, they are not afraid of rejection. (When you stop to think about it, there are some good reasons why we should be rejected!)

It all depends on how we accept rejection. Jesus was rejected— to the point of crucifixion. He is our model. Poverty is the acceptance of rejection for the love of God, arising from faith and hope. Poverty is the acceptance of rejection, but not simply that: Poverty not only accepts rejection, it rejoices in it. That's a much deeper thing.

Poverty is of the heart. It never thinks of itself because it's so busy thinking of others. Poor people have overflowing hearts, ready to share with others. Poverty is this hospitality of the heart. It is not easy, and sometimes it tears you apart.

Poverty is a beggar. He who begs offers the rich an opportunity to share with the poor. Poverty begs not only for itself but for the whole world.

Poverty's middle name is "surrender," total surrender to God. When we surrender we have nothing left, and when we have nothing we are poor. When I try to talk about poverty I see a man with a torn hand—with a nail passing through it—standing at the corner of a street, begging for my heart. I see the Beggar, and I also know that I want to keep my heart for myself. Oh, yes, I am willing to give him some of it, but not all. There's something in us that desires to keep, to possess, and we can't even define it. It seems almost impossible to take the knife of faith, cut it out, and give it to him. But to be able to do that—to mean it and never ask for it back—somewhere, in that act, lies real poverty.

Anawim Yahweh

There is a Hebrew word that is beginning to reach down to the Catholic grass roots. The word is *anawim*. It's a little word. Its sound is musical, soothing, not only to the ear but to the mind, heart and soul of man.

Where did it come from? Who fathered and mothered it? Who brought it forth? It could be said that it is the child of great suffering and of the unshed tears of strong men. It was born from them—yet it has existed for centuries! Its Father really was God himself. It first saw the light of day in the bible, in the Old Testament. It grew up and matured in the New Testament.

Where did it come from? It came from the ivory towers, the secluded rooms of universities, the quiet libraries of the world. It came from scholars who devoted their whole lives to scriptural research—often against tremendous odds!

Anawim. The poor people of whom Yahweh constantly speaks in the Old Testament through his prophets and his holy ones. *Anawim*. The poor people of whom Christ spoke so luminously in the Beatitudes. *Anawim*. Those for so long imprisoned because the word of God was not given in its fullness.

Anawim. The really poor people who *know* that they are poor. Poor because they are creatures. Poor because they know they are utterly dependent on God. People who intuitively, if not intellectually, understand that all things are in Christ and that there is nothing outside of Christ.

Anawim. The poor people who are also holy, who are also wise. How we all need to become the *anawim,* we who rely almost exclusively on ourselves. We who measure ourselves by what we can produce or by the status we can achieve. Not only do we thus reduce ourselves to things which can be weighed and measured, but we imagine we are the sole creators of our technological age.

Anawim. Oh, to become one! To become the poor people of God who "lean" on God, as the scriptures say. Who among us realizes that everything that is, everything we have, comes from God? Who among us rejoices in this poverty which is true riches because it is the knowledge of who he is and who God is?

Anawim. The people who lean on God. This is the reality that will heal the world. To be poor, one must know who God really is. That knowledge, and that knowledge alone, will restore the tranquility of God's order on the earth and among men.

For then God will be able to work through us; we shall not be tempted by the eternal apple. We shall not desire to be like gods. Because we will know with a knowledge given us by the Holy Spirit that we have a loving God, a God who redeemed us, and that we now live in the resurrected Christ. We shall know clearly that in him we live and move and have our being, and that the Father, Son and Holy Spirit dwell in us.

Then we shall see the full splendor of the *anawim,* the poor people who are filled with the Lord of creation, the Lord of love, the resurrected Christ. Then the *anawim* can give him to the world and restore that world to its Savior.

Leaning on God

Much of the talk about "poverty" these days seems to be part of the great hunger of man for God, for the Absolute. At the same time, it seems that men are asking themselves a question that should have been asked a long time ago: "Why, in this modern world, with all its technological development, why is there such a tremendous gap between the developed and the underdeveloped nations? Why, within the affluent nations themselves, is there such an immense gap between the well-to-do and the poor?"

All the discussions about poverty seem to center around two major points. The first is a search for the essence of the beatitudes, especially the one, "Blessed are the poor in spirit, for theirs is the kingdom of heaven." The search for the meaning of these words is deep and constant in our modern society.

Secondly, the search revolves around the question of the terrible inequality among men, the financial and intellectual inequality as well as the grinding poverty of hunger and destitution. This second aspect of poverty concerns not only the Christian but the atheist, the pagan, and the humanitarian as well.

For us Christians, these two aspects of the question of poverty are inseparable. Unfortunately, in discussions, its essence is often missed. It is missed because most of the attention is focused on *personal poverty*, the stripping of goods, the going into the ghettos of the world, and the identification of oneself with the destitute.

Truly this is part of the answer, but not all. Mere physical poverty of this kind is a sort of kindergarten stage where this virtue is concerned. One must go deeper into its essence before embracing a somewhat romantic idea of poverty.

What is the essence of poverty? Where do we start? We should start with ourselves, realizing that true poverty is first and foremost an acknowledgment, a realization of *who we are*. We are creatures, meaning, in the Christian context, that we have been created by God and are totally dependent on him. As we saw above, we are the *anawim*, "the poor men of Yahweh," the "poor men of the beatitudes." To be an *anawim* is to be a person who knows that he is a creature, that he depends totally on God. It is to be a person who "leans" on God, knowing that without God he can do nothing.

This admission of dependence demands great faith in our times, and a flaming charity—charity to oneself, in this case. Among the ways of loving ourselves is this acceptance of our poverty which acknowledges that we are totally dependent on God, and which acts, therefore, always according to his will.

But to act according to God's will, one must empty oneself of all self-centeredness, selfishness, egotism. Positively, one must have a listening heart that is free, poor, one that listens to the quiet voice of God and follows it.

This is the essence of poverty and the fruit of faith and charity. If one possesses this poverty, then all the problems regarding poverty will be easier to solve. In all things spiritual we must always begin with ourselves, and not with the other fellow. If we can give an example of the implementation of the gospel, others will follow. Thus when we become aware of the fact that we are totally dependent on God and that true poverty is the acknowledgment of this dependence, then, in that wondrous soil of true poverty of spirit, we will know what to do in all the other problem areas which poverty presents.

Dispossession

Dispossession. What a strange word this is. Today it is haunting many Christians who are looking for the face of Christ. Dispossession. The Greeks had a different word for this same idea. They called it *kenosis*, which means "self-emptying."

Today, all over the world, men are trying to empty themselves in order to be filled with someone else. Along the streets of our cities, young people with shaven heads, in white robes, chant the name of "Krishna." Other men and women, young and old alike, sit cross-legged, Buddha-style. All across the Western world men and women are seeking mystical experiences of all kinds, often dispossessing themselves of many goods and possessions in order to follow their visions.

All around and about us we see young people dispossessing themselves of their belongings. Many of them come from wealthy and middle-class homes, but they choose to wear the clothing of the poor.

They travel across land and sea often with only a roll of bedding and a knapsack. Not to have anything. To be dispossessed. This seems to be the cry of the modern young people.

It appears as if men cannot stand anymore the disparity between rich and poor. It becomes intolerable until one arises and begins the strange pilgrimage of modern man. Restless feet. Restless hearts. Hungry souls. Hungry hearts. Motion. The motion of searching. Searching—for God.

Yes, dispossession is both the key word and the cry of thousands today. The wind and the fire of the Holy Spirit are abroad. Indeed, it is time that we really examine this hunger for dispossession, for it is often a hunger inspired by the fire and the wind of the Spirit.

The basic thing we have to dispossess ourselves of is our self-centeredness and our selfishness—individually, collectively, nationally and internationally. The world cannot remain divided between the haves and the have-nots. It is time for the haves to become for a while the have-nots so as to know what it is to be hungry, to be tired, to have no place to stay. It is time to face ourselves and to get rid of anything in us which impedes us from becoming brothers to one another. For this is the real goal of all the travail of modern man; this is what he is seeking in all his attempts at dispossession.

The Need Not to Have

The gospel is addressed to all—monk, nun, lay person, married or single. St. John Chrysostom reminds us that the monk and the lay person must attain the same heights. Eastern spirituality, incidentally, blurs the difference between the precepts and the evangelical counsels. It is in its call to absoluteness that the gospel addresses itself to all and everyone. The same Father of the Church goes on to say, "When Christ orders us to follow the narrow path, he addresses himself to all men."

So it seems to me that discussions on poverty must plunge into these depths of the human soul and of the gospel. At the moment there is so much confusion about poverty that it is almost creating a scandal in Christian hearts.

To get at the depths of what poverty really is, let us examine this sentence from Paul Evdokimov's *Struggle With God:* "Absence of the need to have . . . becomes *the need not to have.*" Here is the very essence of poverty in all its aspects—spiritual, physical, emotional.

What are we talking about today when we discuss poverty? Do we discuss *my* need, *your* need to *be* loved, to *be* understood, to *be* consoled? I think we often do. We discuss those needs and desire to have them fulfilled. Witness the million and one courses on interpersonal relationships, sensitivity development and what have you!

We have forgotten St. Francis' formula for happiness and fulfillment. He prayed not that he might *be* consoled, but that *he might console* others; not that he should *be* understood, but that *he might understand* others; not that he should *be* loved, but that *he might love* others. It is precisely by such desires that, like Francis, we will achieve the true ends of all our desires.

We could paraphrase our quotation by saying: "Lord, give me not so much the need to have as the need not to have." Are we filled with this need not to have? Are we cleansing our rooms, ourselves, our houses of all the extra things we really don't need? Are we in search of bare walls and simple life-styles, or are we cluttering up our apartments with a thousand gadgets which only add to our feverish activity?

Are our hearts filled with fire, the cleansing fire which strips us of all that is unnecessary? And I don't mean only physically. Physical poverty is only kindergarten in the school of poverty. It is a sort of plowed field preparing for that fantastic and beautiful fruit which is true poverty of spirit.

No wonder St. Francis called poverty his "Lady" and considered her the most beautiful woman in all the world. For when the need not to have really begins to take root in the heart, then we have come to the essence of poverty.

There is a mystery about poverty which God wants to reveal to those who pray and ask for it. Evangelical poverty is the wealth that belongs to all Christians.

Divine Pauper's Bride

In 1970 we celebrated the 40th anniversary of the foundation of Friendship House-Madonna House. I want to go back in time with you to that first day, when, at long last, freed of all possessions, I went into the slums of Toronto on the greatest adventure of my life. It was the adventure of sharing life with God, with the poor and with the world.

As I recall this gift of God, I want to share it with others, with all the people I know and love, so that they too may praise God with me. It truly seems incredible that the Lord had chosen me, a stranger in a strange land, to be the foundress of an apostolate. My heart praises the Lord, and it is hard to express what happened to me that first day when I went up to serve the Lord and his beloved, the poor.

Perhaps the best way to share that experience with you is to share a poem I wrote when some of our staff were making their promises of poverty, chastity and obedience. It still sums up for me some of my deepest aspirations and rejoicings.

The candles on the altar flickered, shone. Singing their silent song of love for God . . . and dying of that love . . . in song and flame!

White, immaculate, the altar linens lay wrinkleless upon the table of the Lord. Washed, ironed, laid out by many loving hearts and hands.

Below, the Common Room was festive. Again, white linens graced long tables. Candles. Flowers, and beauty expressed by many things, and gifts, collected, sorted, and arranged by many of the household of God, stood beautiful, mute witnesses to loving hearts.

On the great day priests offered up the Sacrifice of Love, for those who, brought by Love, were giving their love to Love!

Young voices sang with souls and hearts . . . the songs of God . . . the songs of Love!

From far and near, friends, families were there, to share and witness to the joy of those who were this day wedded to Christ the King!

Prostrated, awed, transported to what heaven I do not know, God knows . . . I moved and spoke and sang, and did all that was expected of me to do.

Yet I was far away. I was not there. I walked the slummy street on a dark October day of long ago.

My hands were empty. I entered a small, drab house. The smell of poverty, cabbage, and other cooking of the poor was in the air.

A baby cried somewhere as I walked up a narrow stairway and entered the tiny room.

The windowpanes were gray with dust, so was the day outside. The single bed sagged in the middle. The two chairs were rickety, unsafe-looking. The kitchen table was scarred with ink and grease. The floor linoleum cracked in many places.

No cupboard for the few possessions that I had. Just nails in the crumbling plaster of the wall.

Just nails. And a shelf or two. That was the room I came into. The room I knelt in on that gray October day . . . knelt and pledged my life to God forever and forever!

There was no altar. Candles did not flicker. Neither did they sing their song of flame, of love, and death.

No priests were there to offer the Sacrifice for me. Nor was there any music, for there were no voices, young or old, to sing.

No altar linens, immaculate and freshly ironed by loving hands, were there. But then there was no altar to lay them on.

Nor was a table set for me anywhere. With beauty rare, wrought by loving hands.

No, there was nothing of the sort. Just a poor, shabby room, and I kneeling on a cracked linoleum floor!

Yet, I would not exchange that day for any day today. . .

For well I know: My first promises were likewise my final ones. *And there was music in the air!*

The cries of babies. The shouts of children. The raucous cries of peddlers outside. The sound of traffic. Heavy traffic, that takes a shortcut through the slummy city streets. A woman calling to another across a back fence. The laughter of young people and of a man.

All these sounds blended for me into a music of sheer ecstasy! These were to be "my people." In each my Love made love to me! It was himself who sang that day for me, the exquisite, incredible God-made melodies!

There *was* a priest in my gray room. The Lord of Hosts, who is himself Sacrifice and Victim! The altar? His altar was the world at my door, the one he would make and bring to me in the days to come! All of it was there, that day in my gray, shabby room.

There were tables set. One apart for me. Resplendent in beauty. Set not with man-made things, but God-made ones!

That day I drank from his own Cup of Love. And ate from Plates of Hope. My hands were filled with flowers of Faith. And Zeal shone, a priceless necklace on my throat. *All these, his gifts to me!*

My shabby clothes were gone. I was bedecked in splendor! The gold of Poverty shone like a thousand suns. The silver of Chastity made the moonbeams pale! The jewels his love gave me in that gray room—on that gray October day—beggared the power of man's words!

The room became immense! And a thousand voices sang my wedding to the King!

I know his Mother was there, and she whose name I bear. The rest I could not see, blinded as I was with ecstasy!

Yes! I would not exchange . . . my wedding day to God . . . in that gray shabby room . . . on that gray October day . . . for any other day anywhere!

I praise his Name . . . My heart sings gratitude . . . even as angels sing before his throne, unceasingly!

For behold—the Pauper, who wedded me in a slummy street, a crooked house, a shabby room . . . *was a great king . . . Christ the Lord . . . and I became that day a queen . . . his spouse!*

ALLELUIA!   ALLELUIA!   ALLELUIA!

Forty-four years now! There is a difference between then and now. I praise the Lord for both. Alleluia! Alleluia!

Chapter 6 / *Prayer*

Prayer, the Way to Love

Slowly, slowly, quietly, like a tide coming in, we Christians are beginning to pray again! All across America and Canada people find time to enter into solitude, fasting and prayer in order to meet Christ. This meeting, this confrontation is needed if we are going to change the social, political world which is swiftly rolling to the brink of disaster.

We must meet God! This is quite evident if we really want to meet men. Meeting men individually and collectively is the only fundamentally unifying force in this world. And it is we, the Christians, who must let this force loose upon the world by the witness of our lives.

To be a witness does not consist in engaging in propaganda to convert people, or in stirring them up to movements of hatred and violence against one another. It simply means to live in such a way that one's life would not make sense if God did not exist.

This is the time. This is the hour when every Christian must reflect Christ in his life—be the icon of Christ.

We must live the gospel. In order to do so we must pray for

faith which is the cradle of charity and hope! We must pray and ask God to make us realize that he, the Triune God, lives within us. We must pray that he will give us the strength to engage in the only kind of violence allowed the Christian—the violence against himself, for the scripture says, "Heaven is taken by violence."

To love God with one's whole heart and to love one's neighbor as we love ourselves means also to love ourselves the way God wants us to. It means to follow his words, "By this shall all men know that you are my disciples, that you love one another as I have loved you." It means that we must straighten the paths of the Lord in ourselves so that he can come through, so that all men will know him through us.

Love means to approach our enemies with deep tenderness, compassion and understanding, which are the fruits of true love. Love does not mean the destruction of structures, but participating in restoring them to their original purity. Love means that the time has come to lay down our lives for our friends.

This is the time to realize the mystery of God's touching us, enveloping us, loving us. It is the time to understand that love is the key to the mystery of man, and that in love lies the answer to all our problems.

The gradual understanding of this love will be mysterious, for it will come to us through prayer. The Holy Spirit is speaking to us constantly; so often we do not listen to him. Listening to the Holy Spirit is the essence of prayer. Let us begin!

"Teach Us How to Pray"

If the question were asked: What is the one thing needed for the success of the Church's mission, the answer would be—contemplative prayer.

This answer probably would not be understood. For the whole spirituality of North American Catholicism is limited to the minimum: the keeping of the Ten Commandments. This is certainly a true and good foundation on which to build the house of sanctity, but it is still only a foundation, only a well-plowed field, only the first step to holiness.

Because many have only this foundation, we have the tragic picture of a secularized, neopagan society, whose heart is full of the shadows of materialism. How could it be otherwise? One cannot live in a foundation, nor eat off an unseeded field!

Prayer must become an integrated part of our daily lives, the most important part. Then will our house of sanctity rise high and be well built on the rock of faith. Then will our fields be fertile in the Lord, bringing forth a good harvest.

But in order to have this happen the whole approach of "teaching" in the broadest sense must be changed. In the home, in the school, in the parish, *prayer* must be given full and first place.

Every third-grader knows that prayer is the lifting up of one's mind and heart to God. But there are many ways of lifting. It begins with vocal prayer, the one all of us are so familiar with. It goes on to mental prayer and meditation, a prayer that all too many people are *unfamiliar* with. This "lifting" also includes the prayer of silence, the prayer of the heart, contemplative prayer, unknown to still more people.

How many of us have been taught how to pray? Why this defection on the part of our teachers? Could it be that they themselves do not know how to pray? How can we face a world of A-bombs and H-bombs without our own rightful heritage of *spiritual* weapons? How can we attain the fullness of our Christian vocation, humble as it may be, if we are deprived of the meat of the saints which belongs to us by right?

Why then are we bereft of our heritage? Why are we kept on the pap of the minimum when we are entitled to the strong meat of the maximum? We cannot go on in this era of twilight between two civilizations, one dying and one being born, without the fullness of our spiritual heritage.

You who are appointed by God as our teachers—you fathers and mothers of families, you religious teachers of our many schools, colleges and universities, you parish priests, retreat masters, teach us how to know God better, teach us how to love, *teach us how to pray.*

Only the Poor Can Pray

In order to pray to God the first step is to understand who we are, and that is awfully difficult. We must acknowledge that we are creatures, saved sinners, entirely dependent on God. We must be, as the bible says, *anawim,* the poor people of Yahweh, the poor people of the beatitudes who *know* that they depend on God. We must face ourselves and realize that we cannot exist on our own, that we are *dependent.*

To the proud, this is anathema. We look at ourselves and we say, "I depend on no one"—and suddenly, in the very saying, we realize that we do. This is the beginning of prayer: that we become beggars before God, knowing that even the steps we take are given to us by God.

To begin to pray is to first cleanse our souls of arrogance and pride. In grave humility and as beggars, we come to him who alone can make us princes and kings and queens, not of earthly kingdoms, but of the kingdom of God. When we are thus poor and realize our total poverty, then we can go to Bethlehem and meet the Child who became poor for us.

Is there any human being who does not respond to the cry of a child? Did you ever consider the first cry of the Child Jesus? That was his first message of love to us. When we know that we are poor, we can easily enter Bethlehem and answer that cry. We can easily walk behind the donkey that bears the woman and the Child. If we are poor, we will not hesitate to enter the humble home of Nazareth to take part in the hospitality of Joseph and Mary. The proud and the arrogant look down their noses at simple folk from Nazareth: "Can anything good come from Nazareth?"

If we realize our own poverty we will follow him who had nowhere to lay his head. Prayer is the interpersonal relationship of a poor man with the Poor Man.

If we remain poor and keep following the Poor Man, a change takes place. Up to a point, Christ has consoled *us*. But as prayer deepens it enters the darkness of a fantastic faith, a faith that we have to pray for. The time comes when *we have to console Christ*. For we see him all over the world—in slums, in Park Avenues—committing suicide because of the greed of people.

When we console him our prayer takes on a new dimension. The Son of Man became incarnate that you might console him too, so that in consoling him we might learn to console one another, be tender toward one another. He offered himself as a victim for us before he was on the cross so that we might take him in our arms like Our Lady would take him in her arms.

We follow Christ right to the foot of the cross. Our prayer there becomes dirgelike, and yet, it's a joy! Our pain is purified and our prayer moves into still another dimension: We want to be on the cross because our Love is crucified. A strange thing happens: Our prayer becomes a prayer of joy, a fantastic resting in the heart of God.

Thus from a recognition of our total dependence we are led to a prayer where we realize the Father coming to us, knowing the touch of his hand, a human face reflecting the glorified Christ. Thus does prayer come to a total and final resting place, a unity, a complete union of man with God. The darkness of faith grows light and there is no need for words anymore. There is only a need for rest, as a beloved lies in the arms of her Beloved.

We Need More Prayer

What we need today is more prayer. The people of God are weary of being classified on the right or on the left, weary of hearing about bishops and priests marrying, weary of reading about nuns who are seeking answers to questions that only God can answer.

It is this very weariness that is driving people today to pray as perhaps they have never prayed before. The ordinary, simple, "grass-roots" people are seeking answers to their weariness in prayer, prayer for themselves and prayer for others. The right, the left, bishops, priests, nuns—all are coming to realize deep down what they always knew: that prayer can change things.

Youth is seeking prayer. They are listening to gurus, searching into the ways of India, ancient China, the Buddha, Confucius, Mohammed, the Vedas, the ancient books of the Hindus. Yes, youth is hungrily in search of answers.

What we need today is prayer, prayer that is truly interior, coming from the heart, the prayer of Jesus.

In the West the tendency is to divide life into little compartments. Religious answers are sought from various little boxes like in a post office mailing room. But in the East, there is only one immense prayer, the Liturgy, which in the Eastern mind means the Eucharist.

The Russians and other Eastern Christians believe that every Christian is a contemplative simply by the fact that he was baptized in Christ, died there in Christ, rose in Christ, and that therefore there can be no division between contemplation and action. Our faith is a love affair between God and man. Man contemplates God and loves him. Man looks at man and sees God in him and loves him.

Russian saints used to bow before people in the old days because they saw God in them. They used to call the one they bowed before "my joy" and many other such names which expressed their deep understanding that since the Incarnation there can be no separation between our relation to God and to man. They are one because Christ became man.

It is useless to say either I must go to man in order to find God, or to God in order to find man. They are one, and they are both found in that silent and constant interior prayer that brings us face to face with God and makes us understand what Love is. Love is a Person. Love is the Lord. Alleluia!

But love serves, and so action is inseparable from love. Yes, what the world needs today is prayer. Man needs prayer, needs to listen to the Word speaking through the gospel. It is the Word who lives, the Word who prays.

Prayer and Action

The whole world cries out in agony; it cries out for salvation. Humanity may not know to whom it is speaking or where help will come from. Still it cries out. Jesus is the one who saves. Christians are called to love their brothers and sisters who cry out in agony. But how can they help? How can they bring so many millions to true life?

How can they bring justice and mercy to a twisted and needy world? Precisely by the power of God. Christ has said, "Without me you can do nothing." But if in prayer we are one with him, *we can do everything.*

The real answer to all our modern problems, whatever they may be, is to turn toward God with lifted hands, trusting in his promises and mercy, and moved by love for men. There is no other answer. If a person stands with uplifted hands, as Moses did, then the miracle of true action will take place. It seems so strange that the prostration of prayer, or the dance of prayer, or the rock-stillness of prayer—or whatever form prayer takes—floods the world with action. He who turns his face to God in prayer seems also to be in the eye of the hurricane, the eye of action.

This is the miracle that takes place: by prayer man extends himself. He remains on the mountain but at the same time, by the power of his prayer, he walks on the earth with his towel and his water. Like Christ, he wipes the feet of men in social, political and economic action. You name it, he does it! His prayer brings action.

We must all lead one another to the top of the mountain to pray, because prayer is dynamic, and prayer is holy. It is a contact with God; it is a union with him. As a man grows in union with God he comes to know that it is prayer which includes all righteousness, and from which stems all the goodness that God wants to give mankind.

What is this prayer, what is this union with God, then? It is a man or a woman moved with his or her whole being to communicate with the loving God, to respond to God's great love. This prayer can take on a thousand postures—bouncing up and down, arms lifted in supplication, prostration.

Prayer is sometimes the fantastic movement of a dancer. Sometimes it is stonelike, the stillness of a person utterly immobile, lost in regions that few men reach but which many desire. Prayer is sometimes the babbling brook of a child or like the words of old people. Prayer is the words of men, women and children who know God and so easily talk to him!

These words change into beautiful songs when they reach God. Whether people pray the rosary, offer petitions for relatives or the needs of the world, they are caught up in something greater than themselves, indeed, something that is cosmic: The whole universe is bowing down in adoration to God, and those who pray and love him join in that adoration.

God is the only way. There is only one way to lead men to God: teach them to pray and pray for them.

Prayer and Wholeness

We should certainly be concerned about the problems of the world—people around the world who are hungry, poor, the victims of injustice. Perhaps the word is not "concerned" but "tormented." We should be so concerned, so tormented by the plight of the world that we almost become the "other."

How can we identify in this profound, total manner with humanity, or rather incarnate this humanity into ourselves? There already is much involvement; there is even much real concern. Many speak of justice and seek through all possible means to secure it for oneself and for others.

But in all this concern there is much confusion, much chaotic thinking. It seems that many have forgotten that justice is always the child of love. Justice without love is bitter, cold, seldom healing or restoring. Justice without love is often harsh even when it presents real truths.

Love is a Person, Love is God. Where God is, there is love. We try to cut God up into pieces, into part justice and part love. In the reality of daily living one cannot give one without the other.

It is evident these days that we are trying to give justice without love. We try to give truth abstractly as if it only came from books and men's minds. In a word, we have divorced our heads from our hearts. How can we bring the two together so that mankind can be given what it needs with a tremendous love, a love which holds justice on the platter of humility, another name for truth? In order to make such a connection, men must pray.

There is much writing today about prayer. Some say we can only pray "horizontally." Others speak mostly of "vertical" prayer. Here again we have the same problem: the desire to analyze a mystery —for prayer is a mystery, as God is a mystery. We need to connect vertical and horizontal prayer and stop analyzing it! These two dimensions enter into all things.

These two dimensions of prayer were part of the prayer life of Jesus. The scriptures tell us often that he would leave the crowds and go away by himself and pray. These instances are indications of his "vertical" prayer to his Father. They are so numerous as to become almost repetitious.

What about his "horizontal" prayer? His horizontal way of praying was as a carpenter with his tools and wood. He prayed as a member of the community of Nazareth, his community with Mary and Joseph, and with the larger community of the people in Palestine with whom he mingled during his years of preaching and teaching. All these were "horizontal" prayers in which he not only led men to his Father but saw the face of his Father in all men. In Christ's life as in ours, vertical and horizontal lines constantly meet.

Houses are built vertically and horizontally. So is the Mystical Body of Christ. So is the house of our own mind and the house of the heart. These houses constantly remind us of the God-man who came to us vertically and lived with us horizontally, and thus lifted us vertically to the Father.

Yes, of course, we should be concerned about the problems of the world. We should be tormented about them and passionately desirous of bringing to the people love, truth, justice and peace. But in order to do so we must believe in him who is the Prince of Peace, who said he is the Truth, who is our reconciliation, and who is Love itself. We must pray to him constantly in a "vertical" way to give us the strength to do and to pray "horizontally" as he did.

Contemplation and Renewal

Question upon question seems to fill the minds of Catholics today. Hidden away in some dark depths of our souls in the past, now they clamor and crowd us, they whisper and shout for answers, often tormenting our souls almost beyond endurance.

What are we to do? Everything seems to be in flux. Uncertainty and changes confront us on all sides. We are like a boat unmoored and without oars, seemingly afloat at the whim of a thousand currents we never suspected were there.

In the midst of this turmoil of mind, soul and heart, why not return to the primary, basic, simple and fundamental verities of our faith? Why not just call on the Lord in deep faith and ask him to walk once again on the troubled waters, the stormy waters that rage within us so powerfully?

But one must prepare oneself for that "calling" and that "asking." Throughout the scriptures, both the Old and the New Testaments, this preparation always took the form of prayer and fasting. Let us then lift these two arms. This is the time for us to go into the desert as did the prophets of old; as Christ did too.

How does modern man go into a desert? In actual fact, there are few deserts left. But a few can be found, even in our complicated, technological age and culture, where almost all quiet places are taken over by sprawling cities and suburbs.

It would be good if every Catholic could spend some time in a real quiet desert place, geographically speaking. But it seems there isn't enough available space for all of us on this North American continent.

But there is one desert into which everyone can go. That is the desert of silence and of quiet in his own heart. There is a Russian saying that states very simply and directly, "Every Christian must be a contemplative whilst living in the noise and the hurly-burly of the world."

The typical modern man might smile at this seemingly simple solution, at this childlike (or perhaps, to him, childish) answer. Yet, if we stop just for a moment to think about it, we will see that this answer *is the preparation needed to be able to call on God to come and walk on the stormy, raging waters of our minds and souls.*

We can create silence in our hearts. We should. Contemplation is simply a question of loving. No one yet questions the fact that God loved us first! Few question the fact that our faith is a love affair, that we should love God back, and that we should love our neighbor as Christ loved us. All of us give intellectual assent to these basic verities.

Now, people can be busy while still keeping the people they love present to them. A woman can be a nurse, taking care of her patients with great efficiency, yet, in her mind and heart be deeply united with her husband. She may be a typist and be immersed in work, while the eyes of her heart behold the countenance of her beloved.

What human beings can do when they love one another, a Christian can do with the Tremendous Lover who is the Lord. That is the desert we must go to in order to prepare ourselves to ask God to answer our questions, the million and one questions which plague us. When he comes into our hearts, then we will be questionless, for then we shall know the truth. He is truth, and he will set us free.

Yes, let us stop the noise of our minds and hearts. Let us go into the desert within ourselves and prepare our souls for his coming. Then everything else will be given to us.

Poustinia

Gurus, wise men from the East, have captured the imagination of millions in Canada and America. Magazines are filled with articles and pictures about them and their followers.

This hunger of men for God continues to grow. It flows into a thousand channels. What are we Christians doing about it? What are our answers to this search that has grown so fantastically since the growth of technological development?

Even in Madonna House we feel the pressure of this hunger. We have only found one answer—one tiny, strange answer that may grow into one of the answers. What is it? *Poustinias.**

Poustinia is a Russian word for desert or hermitage. We had built a log cabin for ourselves, never thinking of it as an answer to anything. We built it because much of our work is in the market-place, and we felt the need for entering the desert once in a while. Now we have 14 of these cabins. If the influx of people continues, we shall have to build many more cabins where people can come to rest in the great silence of God, content to read his word, to fast, and to pray. This is our Christian answer to the gurus, our way of ful-filling the hunger for God.

We cannot build hundreds of cabins for the many people who will want to leave the noisy city for the silence of God—the laden tables for the fast that will bring them closer to the hungry of the world. But perhaps this is straw in the wind, a suggestion that others will pick up. The Church always has an answer. This is only one of them. There must be others.

The Speech of Silence

The charismatic movement has brought into focus the gift of tongues, one of the gifts of the Holy Spirit mentioned in the scriptures. But do you know who speaks in all languages? Silence.

Have you ever looked into the eyes of a person who has looked into the eyes of God and realized that you understood one another? Deep and profound are the wells of silence. It is necessary not only for communication; it is necessary also for our peace.

There is unpeace in our hearts. Why? Because we are not silent, we have not lifted our hearts to God. We have not communicated with him. We have not taken that inner counsel with the Other, that strange counsel that flows from the union of love.

* See my book, *Poustinia* (Ave Maria Press, Notre Dame, Ind., 1975).

How many of us are silent enough to be able to really listen to another? Peace is a way of listening to others. When one is really listening while another is talking, they begin to understand each other. We don't know how to listen because we have no inner peace, no inner silence of mind and heart. Silence is the way to peace and it flows from love. Only those who are capable of loving can be silent.

It is not easy to be silent. Man begins his journey inward to meet God who dwells within him. Jesus said that his Father and the Holy Spirit would come and dwell within us. That's what the journey inward is all about. Once I meet the Trinity, then my silent communication with them will transform me into the icon of Christ.

Icon means image. I shall bring forth out of the depth of silence —out of this silent communication—the likeness of God. Isn't this what all our hearts hunger for? It is. It is for this that we really crave. St. Augustine has said that our hearts are restless until they rest in God.

True silence is always restful. Silence is a cradle. It was the cradle of the Incarnation. There was a great and awesome silence when God was born. There was a great and awesome silence over the whole earth for that moment. If we continue our inward journey, we too can become cradles for the Child. We must make cradles of our hearts for any who wish to come and rest in them like children.

There is no man or woman living who deep down doesn't long to become a child. Jesus expressed this secret longing when he said, "Unless you become as little children, you shall not enter the kingdom of heaven." This is why my favorite prayer is, "Lord, give me the heart of a child and the awesome courage to live it out as an adult." Silence prepares a crib, a creche for the tired man.

Silence is more than a cradle; it is an inn. There was a good Samaritan. He picked up off the road a man besieged by robbers. Who of us is not besieged by robbers? Who of us does not need the inn of another's heart where everything is peace and rest and silence? This is what silence can do for others once we have understood what it is—the greatest form of speech, the highest type of communication, the quickest way to peace, a cradle for others, an inn for the tired and the weary. All this silence will do if we fall in love with God.

We need to become the icons of Christ, because what does the world need most of all? It needs to touch God. I used to ask my mother, "Mommy, how can I touch Jesus?" She said, "Touch me." In my own silence and in the silence of others I will realize that I can touch Jesus. Silence is the key to many secrets of God. Why don't we ask him to give us this key?

Chapter 7

Gifts & Virtues

Faith

What is faith? Some say they have lost it. Some hunger for the first taste. Some are indifferent to whether they have it or not. Others fight against it, hate it, and want to destroy it in others.

What is faith? A Catholic can easily answer from early catechetical instructions in childhood. Faith is a free gift from God, given to a person at Baptism. A Catholic will say too that no one can really acquire faith by his own efforts. He will repeat over and over again that it is indeed a free gift from God.

Yes, faith is a free, loving gift of God to man. Faith is the cradle of love and of hope. But this gift given to us at Baptism can grow, must grow, must be incarnated into our lives, must become part of us, must become, like breathing, an utterly integral part of us.

How can it become all these things? By prayer. God never refuses a prayer for the deepening and the growth in faith. Prayer is the food that will make faith grow, strengthen it, root it with deep and lasting roots into the hearts of men.

Faith grows by living it out. Faith is a pilgrimage toward the

Absolute. Faith gives every Christian sandals and a pilgrim's staff and bids him to arise and go in search of him whom every Christian longs for—God.

Faith appears to be blind sometimes but in reality it sees very deeply. It alone can walk in utter darkness. It alone can fold the wings of the intellect when necessary and open them when it needs to. Chasms, abysses, steep mountains present no problem or difficulty to faith. On the contrary, all of life—the pains, sorrows, joys symbolized by these chasms—becomes its food and its nourishment. Faith grows until it leaves all darkness behind and walks like a child bathed in the light of God's love.

No one can keep or hide faith for himself alone. It will escape and extend itself to others. Faith never walks alone, but always walks with love and hope. Faith can be transmitted by words, but it is best communicated by actions. Faith cries out to be lived, to be incarnated, incarnated in love. For love is a Person, love is God, and faith is his gift to mankind.

The hands of faith are filled with gifts for those who embrace her. Gifts of peace, love, joy and strength. Gifts of courage and laughter. Faith is a child who smiles at theologians and at the wisdom of men. Faith invites them to come and play with God.

Touching Christ

Faith is received on our knees. We have too little of it. We have to pray for it because, whether we realize it or not, the immensity of this gift overwhelms us.

The majority of us look at ourselves and say, "He made us in his image! Equal to his image! Heir with his Son! This just can't be! He hasn't looked into my heart. He doesn't know what I'm made of!"

We say those silly things because we are upset, because our evaluation of ourselves is very poor. We haven't looked at ourselves with the merciful, tender, compassionate eyes of God. And so, half of the time we walk in despair, and the fruit of faith—the ability to realize that God is both in our midst and in us—pales and sometimes disappears.

The Father, having given us the fantastic gift of faith in him, wanted to make it secure—something like crossing the *t* and dotting the *i*. He sent his Son. He sent his Son so that from shaking faith we might pass on to firm faith.

We are so much like children. We have to touch things! So, once upon a time, the Second Person of the Most Holy Trinity walked this earth. He died for us. He brought us a new covenant, a new pact with the Father. After he died he was raised and faith exploded like a thousand stars and suns. Love carried a platter with faith on it and presented it to man.

We try to pit our peanut brains against the mystery of faith. We use our well-manicured hands to try and tear apart the veil of faith. We want to see if we can weigh it, measure it. We want to define what faith is.

Faith eludes us if we approach it in this way. The only way to approach faith is on our knees—through prayer. There is one thing God the Father will never refuse: growth in faith. This is the time when we should be prostrate before him, imploring, crying out for faith.

We should ask not only for a faith in God but also for faith in man. Nonbelief is suicidal. Either I enter upon a life of faith in God and man, or I will enter upon a life of despair. There is an enlargement, a pulsating, fantastic fire that enters the heart of man once he believes.

Deep in the heart of faith which is a gift of God lies the fantastic understanding of who we are. Who are we? We are people of the towel and the water. Jesus washed the feet of his apostles with a basin of water and dried them with a towel. Faith must make of us people of the towel and the water. Such a faith knows no difficulty. Faith knows no barriers.

Faith liberates. If I am free to love and free to hope, what more do I want of life? Faith makes me one with Christ. Now I act like him; now I am he. That is the ideal. Faith is taking hold of Christ's hand. But to take his hand you must remember that it is pierced. Faith tells me that I am going to Golgotha, because that is the only way I can achieve the fullness of the understanding of faith.

Once I am cruciform, once I accept the cross, it falls away from me. Now I accept pain as if it were a joke, or a song. Now I accept all that comes with a joy beyond understanding. Now all men are my brothers and each one is my joy. All this happens when the Trinity bends over you in Baptism, when you enter the death and resurrection of Christ and come forth a Christian.

Yes, we pray for faith on our two knees, even though we know that one day it will fall away along with hope. But rising out of faith and hope will be that shining flame of the love of God. But we had to go through faith to find him.

Diaspora Faith

This is the age of faith, not the great age of faith of the Middle Ages, but the age of the faith of those living in the *diaspora*.

We Christians who believe in the Lord Jesus Christ as the Second Person of the Most Holy Trinity, born of a virgin, who died, rose and will come again in glory, we must cry this gospel with our lives. Our age of faith demands the incarnation of the gospel. Nothing short of this will do. Oh, we can preach it with our lips, but only after we have preached it with our lives!

Perhaps this new age of faith also demands martyrdom. A strange kind of martyrdom. A white martyrdom. A martyrdom of ridicule by one's peers, by the young and the old. A martyrdom of loneliness. In the diaspora Christians will often have to walk alone amidst uncomprehending crowds. They will have to be ready to be not only ridiculed but rejected with contempt.

This is the age of diaspora faith, a faith that must be lavishly sown into the four winds against all odds, especially against the forces of the intellect. We live in a technological society intoxicated with the exploits of landing on the moon and with mechanical gadgets of all kinds. It's a society which demands that everything be measured, weighed, programmed and put into neat little mental cubbyholes.

In the midst of all this scientific achievement one must sow the seeds of faith into the souls of men. In each man there is still a field, a small knoll, a garden that longs for reseeding. Màn, in his deepest being, does not want to be put into a cubbyhole. He needs and wants the open spaces where he can be himself, and breathe! He longs especially for the open spaces of the spirit, the spaces where God dwells, for it is he for whom he hungers.

It is the age of faith, not so much for those who have never had it, but for those who have lost it, wrapped it up somewhere deep within themselves, buried it so deeply that they have forgotten that they ever had it, or where they have buried it.

It is up to us Christians to tell them by our lives that God is with us. It is for us Christians to be a light to their feet and to help put those feet on the path of rediscovery of faith. It is the path of prayer both for them and for us.

For us, so that we will have the courage to recognize that this is the age of faith in the diaspora, prayer is especially necessary. We are called to sow faith by incarnating it in our lives, by living the gospel, by praying and by becoming pilgrims—pilgrims with an eternal lantern in our hands, the lantern and light of Christ for men.

Theology

Perhaps I shouldn't even try to explain my relationship with theology. Yet, at times I have a great desire to do so.

Perhaps I should start by saying that I love theology, for I love God and I love everything that has ever been spoken or written about God. I never tire of reading or conversing about God. I should say that I have taken courses in philosophy, ethics and logic, and that I have taken a course in theology, four years of scholastic theology.

One thing I loved about it tremendously was St. Thomas Aquinas and how he wanted to burn his books once he "saw God." Yes, at the end of his life Thomas really *knew*. He knew what God himself had taught him. It reminds me also of the story about the Hindu monk who requested a priest come and instruct him in the teachings of the Catholic faith. After two hours of listening the Hindu monk bowed low and said, "Thank you, Father. You have filled my head with beautiful thoughts, but you have left my heart empty."

This story brings back to mind my own reactions to my studies in theology. I began to understand that in the perspective of the Eastern Church, theology is essentially an *experience*. "An experience is knowledge which comes from beyond all concepts. It is this contemplative knowledge by participation which the Fathers called theognosis.

"In other words, God-knowledge. Theology is a communication with the life of God, a knowledge flowing from participation of God in man who is the image of God. To do theology means to agree to live this revealed truth (without necessarily speaking about it); and if one must speak, at all costs to try to relate the content (often inexpressible) of this communion with God.

" 'If you truly pray, you are a theologian, and if you are a theologian you truly pray.' This definition of theology by Evagrius of Pontus expresses the reality of the Eastern Church's life and of certain great spiritual teachers of the West."

Yes, that is what I thought too. It seems to me that he is a theologian who knows how to keep silence and let God speak. He is a theologian who enters into God's ineffable presence so as to be able to enunciate and translate it through the forms of this world. He is a theologian who also manifests this presence in active love for man and works in union with others for the realization of the kingdom.

"To do theology is, for the Eastern Church, to go out in search of God; it is a search which leads inevitably to the discovery of man. It is a search that, while employing reason, leads to an encounter on the other side of reason. 'For concepts create idols, and only wonder lays hold of something' (Gregory of Nyssa). 'God is not above,' said St. Isaac the Syrian, 'he is ahead, in the anticipation of the encounter.'

"To 'do theology' is to participate in the living reality of the Christ who by the Spirit offers himself to us every day in the private conversation of prayer, in the offering of the Eucharist, in the words of the bible, in the assembly of the brethren, and in everyman, in every man whom he calls us to serve.

"To 'do theology' is, in the final analysis, a love affair between God and man. To do theology is also to admit that the true revolution for a Christian, that which comes first and which justifies and gives meaning to all the others is evangelical metanoia."

These excerpts from an article came to my attention as I was meditating on theology and seemed to express everything that I felt about it.

Yes, to me, theology is to go in search of God; and every time I venture forth I find people, each one dearer than the next. When I pray, the faces of each turn into his face. Theology is such a simple thing. You don't need to go to big courses and study the writings of lots of theologians who seem to contradict one another. No. All you and I have to do is "to go out in search of God."

The Theology of the Pastors

I was having a conversation once with some priests and nuns who had just finished a course in pastoral theology. They were excited, yet at the same time their voices contained a question mark; as if, having drunk of all this knowledge, they found it lacking in something they could not define. I was puzzled at their being puzzled, for just before they came I had been praying the 23rd Psalm, which seemed to me to contain the essence of all pastoral theology.

"Shepherd" means "pastor," but our modern age is not very familiar with shepherds. A pastor is one who, like a shepherd, takes care of his flock. It all seems rather simple to me. If one went through the gospel this whole matter of pastoral theology would be lying in the palm of one's hand.

"The Lord is my shepherd, and there is nothing I lack." The first thing shepherds need to realize is that they are the *anawim* of the Lord, and that they lack nothing. This is the essence of pastoral theology. When the priest, the pastor, the shepherd understands this, he will be transformed. Once a shepherd knows who he is—that of himself he is nothing, that he is totally dependent on God—his voice changes, the sheep hear it clearly, and follow wherever he leads.

In the East, as most everyone knows, the shepherd walks ahead, and the flock follows behind. Yes, if the shepherd knew he was totally dependent on God, and knew why he was a shepherd, his very voice would be filled with immense tenderness and compassion, and the sheep would follow.

"In meadows of green grass he lets me lie. To the waters of repose he leads me; there he revives my soul." God first brings his shepherds to the green meadows of the mystery of himself and lets them lie there. Men who lie in the green meadows of the Lord are not too concerned about what is going to happen to them. They are immersed, engulfed, absorbed in a total faith, an utter trust and confidence in him.

How long do the shepherds of the Lord lie in the Shepherd's meadows? How long does he let them drink of the waters of his repose that revive their souls? No one can tell, but this is the time when they are being prepared to become true shepherds.

"He guides me by paths of virtue for his name's sake." The pastor also guides his flock by leading them, that is, by preaching the good news to the poor. All the flock is poor. By preaching the good news he guides his flock along the "path of virtue."

So priests, pastors, shepherds preach the good news to the flock in order to bring each one of them into the arms of the Father through Jesus. Here the mystery deepens, because the flock is composed of people—men, women and children. We are dealing with the mystery of God blending in the shepherd and in the sheep.

The Trinity is in the pastor in a very special way. The pastor brings the Trinity to every member of his flock. The shepherd makes us walk a narrow path on the mountain of the Lord, where at every turn things become clearer to us, and the dimensions of God's love—Father, Son and Holy Spirit—become greater. For the priests, the pastors, the shepherds are leading us to the summit of God's mountain where he, we, and the Triune God will be one!

I am a path . . . you are a path. Now, by the grace of the Lord and with the help of his shepherd, I am able to lift my weak hands and begin to build within myself a straight path to the Lord.

"You prepare a table for me in the sight of my foes." The Lord is not only a shepherd, he is also a host. He lays his beautiful table in the midst of the flock. It is his priest who can transform the bread and the wine on that table into God himself to give to all of us our food for the journey which we need for following the Shepherd.

The guests and I stopped talking. I understood what pastoral theology was all about. I thought the best preparation for it was prayer— the prayer of the Eucharist, the prayer of the bible, the prayer of silence. Somehow, quite unconsciously, we had all become silent. The question marks having died, we realized that the Good Shepherd was among us. It was an almost perfect moment. All of us had suddenly and totally forgotten all about pastoral theology, because we had met the Pastor.

The Awesome Gift of Prophecy

Prophecy is one of the gifts of the Holy Spirit. It must be approached as Moses approached the burning bush—without shoes, as the place is holy. As with all the gifts of God to man, it is God who chooses the gift as well as the man.

There are, of course, some people who have more than one gift, but they are very few. The gifts of God, the gifts of the Spirit, are heavy, fraught with deep responsibility. This is because they are never intended merely for oneself, but are always to be used for others.

Anyone can receive the gift of prophecy, if God so wills, but we must remember it is a gift that comes from him and that we ourselves can never bring it forth. Of all the gifts of the Spirit, prophecy is the weightiest. The prophet is like a piece of clay in the hands of God. He has received words from God to give to men!

Those who have received that gift must pray without ceasing, otherwise they will be unable to keep the words that God gives them. The pressure of the Lord will be unbearable without prayer. A prophet is like a tree bent by the wind, perhaps almost to the breaking point—his mouth touched by fire.

Those who receive such a gift should prepare themselves to be reduced to being the refuse of the world. True prophecy is not readily accepted by the men of our times. Modern man does what he wants, when he wants, how he wants. When he encounters a truth he does not want to accept, he is likely to reply with violence. His first reaction is to hit the person uttering the truth.

No one should consider the gift of prophecy a trifling matter. Because of the thousands of contradictions in which Christians live today, it is good for the one who has or thinks he has the gift of prophecy to have a spiritual director. There is no path more illusory than to attribute to oneself the gift of prophecy.

The gift of prophecy is a dangerous one. A person is tempted to attribute to God whatever he says. Then, of course, he will not be a prophet of God but a prophet of the forces of darkness.

Consider a human being who has words of God to pass on to his fellowmen. His tongue becomes a bridge between God and us. He himself becomes almost nonexistent because he is so impregnated with God.

Consider the prophets of old. All of them were afraid. All cried out, "Ah, Lord God! Behold, I do not know how to speak, for I am only a young man. I can only say, 'ah, ah, ah.' "

Sometime, reread the Old Testament and even the New Testament, and see what happened to those who were chosen to be prophets. Most of them were martyred. Today, in the pentecostal movement, it almost seems as if we haven't gone into the immense depths of the seriousness of this gift.

We haven't fully understood that it is truly God compelling us to speak his truths in our modern tongues. Sometimes, in pentecostal gatherings, we treat prophecy too lightly. We don't seem to realize the agony of a prophet. Truly, there is no prophet who hasn't experienced agony.

Prophecy is the word of God given to man in order to be given to other men. But what and who is the word of God? The Word of God is Jesus Christ. The prophet, in a manner of speaking, becomes the word of God. How light, how heavy, is the word of God? Only those who have been called to the true gift of prophecy can answer.

But the burning bush is still in our midst. It always will be. The voice of God will reverberate in the ears of those he has chosen. When we hear such a word we inwardly take off our shoes because the place and the time are holy.

Forgiveness

Forgiveness is one of the urgent spiritual needs and actions of today! Truly there is no use beating about the bush. No use hiding behind rationalizations. No use sharpening our philosophical and theological arguments.

The time is now to *forgive*. Begin with oneself, for one must always begin with oneself. Christians on the North American continent are guilt-ridden. Because of this we often attack the ones before whom perhaps we ought to feel especially guilty, if we're going to feel guilty at all! We do this to get out of the dead-end street to which we have come.

The Lord said, "Love your neighbor as yourself." Which means we must love ourselves first, for we are, in a manner of speaking, our first neighbor.

In order to love, one must forgive. For one cannot love the object of hostility, anger, hatred and unforgiveness. Yes, we must begin with forgiving ourselves as our Father in heaven forgives us.

Simply, most sincerely and with grave humility, we must acknowledge our sins before ourselves. This means that we have to go into the very depths of our souls and bring them, our faults, into the light. Then, after having begged forgiveness for them from God, we must forgive ourselves.

How often have we gone to confession, been forgiven, but remained uneasy, tragically still feeling guilty of those very sins we have just confessed to God. We do not really trust either his love or his forgiveness.

This is the hour in which we must begin to understand that we must love one another, and that means first forgiving ourselves and everybody else!

It might seem utterly idiotic, stupid, irrelevant to be writing about the command "to love your neighbor as yourself" by imploring everyone to begin by forgiving. Yet, with the world in shambles, where greed shows its face openly and does not even try to hide, where evil means are used to ensnare and subject man to other men, where all dams seem to be breaking loose, where the sticky, black waters of evil rise higher and higher across our cities and countries, what else is there left to talk about but this command of the Lord? But that means forgiveness. That demands mercy and compassion. "Blessed are the merciful, for they shall obtain mercy."

It is true that forgiveness, mercy and compassion may and probably will lead to that other truth uttered by Christ, "Greater love has no man than he lay down his life for his friends." But wouldn't it be wonderful to die trying to forgive and love, rather than to die with hatred in one's heart?

Let us ask Mary, the Mother of God and men, who loved and forgave—forgave the race that killed her Son—to teach us how to pray, how to love, how to forgive.

Collective Sin

Is sin always an individual occurrence? Is it possible for there to be a collective, corporate sin? Looking down the long corridor of history one can find many instances of collective, corporate sin in which a group of people, sometimes whole countries, participated.

The individual, under such circumstances, might even appear to be sinless. Yet, participating in a collective, corporate sin he may be guilty because he has lost the ability to judge between good and evil.

All who participated collectively in Hitler's Third Reich madness were guilty of a sin greater than any individual sin could be. They didn't rob anyone. They didn't seem to harm anyone, as individuals, that is. But somehow or other they agreed, they followed, they were involved in the heinous sin of exterminating six million Jews. Somehow they also participated in a mad orgy of trying to conquer the world. This was a collective sin, a corporate sin, for which a whole nation must atone, and is atoning.

So many people lately bring forth, for their exoneration, the fact that some superior, some commander-in-chief has ordered them to do this or that. They claim they were not responsible for what they did. Theirs was not a sin; on the contrary, it was an act of obedience, far removed from sin. As a soldier, to be involved in a mass killing of women and children because of an "order from headquarters" is to be involved in a corporate, collective sin. The order should have been disregarded, even at the price of one's own life if need be.

Each person involved in the tragedy of Watergate apparently didn't think he was committing individual, personal sins. The money they collected was for the "party." The bugging perhaps was considered justified to help the "cause." But the cloud that hangs now so unhappily over the United States is the cloud of collective, corporate sin. It is time we should recognize this collective kind of sin, especially in politics and government. We cannot ignore it. If we do, we must also submit to its consequences. We shall be sinning with the others.

The tragedy of Watergate is what happened to the integrity of the individuals involved. Like so many of Hitler's men, they simply "obeyed." They obeyed in spite of the fact they sensed that obedience in this case was a grave sin, a collective sin against God and the nation.

This time after Watergate is a time for prayer. Let all of us, American or non-American, pray for the United States. Collective, corporate sin is marring the nation's reputation for charity and compassion, undermining its Constitution and outraging its democracy. Indeed, this is a time for prayer.

Just Anger

At what point in the hidden depths of a man's heart and soul does just anger begin? At what point does a Christian lift the cords of that anger to chase the moneylenders out of the temple? When does a man reach the breaking point and begin to speak with words of fire and truth to a mighty and powerful one of the world?

There is such a thing as just anger. We see it in the gospel.

Christ did pick up cords and chase the moneylenders out of the temple; he did call the Pharisees and Sadducees vipers and whitened sepulchers.

I personally know the terrible storms of anguish when just anger shakes a person like a fever, like a fierce cold wind which makes a man's teeth rattle.

I knew it in the slums of Toronto during the Depression when long queues of hungry men waited in line in front of our store. We were without food ourselves. Our begging did not bring us anything to share with them. Yet, on the evening of that day, I was invited to lecture to a Catholic audience in some swanky hotel where men and women were eating rich and costly food which they did not need to eat.

I knew it in the Harlem of America where I spent ten years. My one desire there was to have black skin. I traveled across the vast continent of the U.S.A. crying out into the indifferent and cold white faces the pain of the Negro. I didn't care when I was almost lynched in the South. I was glad. I didn't care about the tomatoes, eggs and other things that were thrown at me occasionally by some audiences. I didn't care about the open and often hidden persecution to which I was subjected. My just anger was too great for the caring. I prayed that I might die for my brother the Negro, but obviously I was not worthy of martyrdom. Still, the just anger shook me.

I cannot deny that I often used words like cords, and that very often, upon returning to my bedbug-infested room in Harlem, the temptation to use the talents of words to arouse the Negro to violence would come upon me.

I am still filled with this just anger, because the face of poverty, the face of injustice, the face of man's inhumanity to man is still before me everywhere I go. It is present in the rural slums of Canada, in the vast North with its Indian minorities, in the underdeveloped countries.

At what point does this just anger, this searing pain which never leaves me, at what point does it cross over an imaginary line and burst into the kind of violence that we see all around us?

Who will answer me? Who will give me some guidelines? I, who consider myself an apostle of peace and nonviolence, I am shaken. Christ's answer is always a paradox. I need someone who will clarify this paradox for me. He says, "He who takes up the sword will perish by the sword." Then, a little later, he says, "If you are hit on one cheek, turn the other"—but then he picks up cords and scourges people in the temple! He also uses words like swords!

How long is it possible for a Christian to watch the face of the poor being ground into the dust by the rich? How long is it possible to watch governments of affluent nations dole out mere fistfuls of grain to the hungry when granaries are bursting? How long is it possible to watch well-off people gorge themselves on surplus food, then pay ridiculously high fees to doctors to help them reduce, and all the while half of the world is starving? To whom shall I turn for an answer to these questions? Just anger is a devouring fire in thousands of Christian hearts and minds.

I have only one answer for myself: unceasing prayer, fasting and a fiat to God to remain crucified on the cross of tense, just anger. I feel safe on that strange wooden cross. For he who is nailed to it cannot succumb to the temptation of violence, for temptation it really is. A crucified person can only hang there, and slowly die for those with whom he identifies.

Perhaps that is the only answer: suffering on that cross. Such people cannot do anything but die. They die so that hope may be born in the hearts of the poor. They die so that love may blossom in the hearts of the rich—a love that will reach to the very bottom of the poverty of their brethren.

Chastity and the Gospel

In many ways we have really forgotten what chastity is all about. Jesus Christ came on earth but he did not marry. He set up a pattern, an ideal. There are people who are chaste in marriage, and there are others who are chaste for the kingdom of God. But to everyone the commandment of the Father was directed: Anyone who looks with lust at a person of the opposite sex has already committed adultery in one's heart.

Christ put the whole matter of chastity in the context of the heart, not of the mind. You and I can spend days and weeks and months rationalizing things away, but the gospel doesn't rationalize. The gospel goes straight to the heart of the matter. No one demands celibacy of you if you do not wish to practice it, but the gospel always demands that relationships with the opposite sex be established on a loving foundation.

But it goes deeper. Chastity demands purity of heart, for the pure shall see God. When you see God your respect and love for your neighbor begin to become like that of the heart of Christ. In marriage, two people enter the most glorious adventure that man and woman can enter *provided* they love each other, *provided* the foundation of their coming together is not lust. Love is in the heart, not in bodily functions.

The pure of *heart* shall see God. That means that we should see God in everyone. Once I see God in them I respect them, I love them. I will not use that person for my own end, i.e., that *I* might be satisfied physically or emotionally—and then drop the person like a rag doll when I am through fulfilling *my* needs.

What is lacking in the relationships between men and women today is *depth*. The common attitude is, "what can I get" from the other person, instead of what can I *give*. Even in giving, there is misunderstanding. We think that if we enter into unions with others we are God's gift to them! We are, but only when we think first of the other person, and not of ourselves.

Deep and profound are God's words on chastity, and a chaste life has fantastic heights and depths. Who of us has not taken our hat off to a chaste person? When we see a chaste person something happens to us, something that we cannot explain. We think of God. Such people are like signposts pointing toward the Parousia, the second coming of the Lord.

Celibacy is the absence of sexual relations between men and women. It is the relinquishing of one of the most precious things that man has—the power of procreating, begetting, nurturing children. Perhaps the young priest, the night before his ordination, sees the children that will never be born from him, the woman who will never lie at his side. Perhaps the nun does the same thing sometimes, and we here at Madonna House; I'm sure we do. But then we look this gift straight in the eye and we lift it up to the Lord, like a chalice.

Of course, sex will be with us till the day we die. Sex was created by God the Father and raised to tremendous heights of dignity by God the Son. It is a difficult thing to give it up. But it was difficult to hang on a rough cross for three hours too. It was difficult to be scourged, to be pushed around. Christ did that for you and me. No one is stopping us from getting married, just as no one stops us from loving. We give it up out of love.

If we are in love with God, we will not spoil the image of God in others. It is always out of love that we respect the gift of sex in another. It is a precious gift. It is not something to be treated lightly.

The Dimensions of Solitude

Today, everybody wants to seek salvation in *solitude*. While this is a very wonderful idea, does anybody ever reflect that the Trinity kind of disagrees with it? The Second Person of the Trinity became *man*. When I was in the Holy Land I didn't see much seeking after solitude on the part of the people. They were carpenters, upholsterers. Everybody was yelling and rushing around. Venders were crying out their wares. I imagine it was much the same in the time of Jesus Christ.

For many years he seemed to have led this kind of life, and then he started preaching. Well, the poor man, he didn't have much time to get away and pray then! He tried to get away in boats; he tried hiding. Occasionally he managed some solitude, but not too often. The moment you start preaching like Jesus Christ preached, the world comes around you and immediately keeps on following you. When you have a whole nation, or at least an immense crowd, following you, you don't have much real solitude.

But he did have a deep solitude—on the cross. There he had solitude indeed. Yet, even there there were a lot of people yelling this and that, people, especially those he had helped the most, yelling that he was no good. He also had deep solitude in the garden of Gethsemane when he wept bloody tears. How his solitude was "peopled" by us from the beginning to the end!

What exactly is solitude? There are so many aspects to it. Real solitude is love. Instinctively we leave the newlyweds alone in solitude. Love, to express itself, needs solitude. Solitude is first of all a dimension of the heart; then it expresses itself in the act of being alone. But before you think of entering any Trappist or Trappistine hermitage, your heart must love, otherwise you will never be solitary. That is to say, you may be *alone,* but you will know more of what hell is like than heaven! When there is no love, solitude is withdrawal from life and anger at the fact of withdrawal from life.

Solitude is love. As I repeat endlessly, love is the mystery of man meeting God. God loved us before the foundations of the world, and he loves us now. When man turns around to God and loves him, the two mysteries come together and solitude enters the heart. It is a solitude of joy, a solitude of peace, a solitude of tranquility.

Most problems, as time passes in this kind of solitude, fall away. For it is the meeting of the bride and the bridegroom, beginning now and ending, flowering, in death. True solitude is that kind of love— my love relationship with God.

How many of us are in love with God, I mean really in love with God? Most people have had friends of the opposite sex. They know what a thrill it is to wait for the boy or girl at a given place. I have been married twice and I've experienced that kind of thrill. You know something? Those meetings were like pennies compared to the million dollar thrills of waiting for God. Waiting for him, and knowing that he is really there waiting for you!

Solitude with God is a strange thing. You do not go anywhere to be alone unless God calls you there. You stay right where you are and your solitude is a benediction on everyone who meets you. Love is always a benediction. Love is always a joy. Love is always the answer to the thousand and one questions which people ask. Our tragedy is that we don't want to be solitary, which means that we don't want to fall in love with God. He asks too much. When one falls in love with God, one has to go to the solitude of the cross as well.

I'm sure that many people know what I'm talking about when I say that those who are truly solitary within themselves—those who truly love God—reach a stage of immense freedom. They are caught up in a wind that picks them up like leaves in the fall and whirls and twirls them around (for the Lord likes to dance).

For the majority of people, solitude can and should be lived among others, and not in a hermitage. Some are called into physical solitude; the majority are not. The answer to the problems of the world is men and women in love with God and in the solitude of their hearts holding on to both Christ's love and his cross. We who are Christians must show forth this kind of solitude. We must be icons of Christ. He was a carpenter, simple, humble—no big deal! But like him, our whole hearts must pulsate with the solitude of lovers.

Silence, the Deepest Speech

Silence goes hand in hand with solitude. In our modern age our minds are like buzzing bees. We cannot even hear ourselves think. On the other hand, we are so constantly concentrated on ourselves that our ears are plugged, and we cannot listen either. Silence does not dwell in us, and yet it should.

What is silence? Silence has many ramifications or accents. To be silent you have to be recollected. That means you have to "gather yourself up," for we are all fragmented, broken into pieces. Man is fragmented; he doesn't know himself, and he doesn't know his neighbor—and what is worse, he doesn't care to! But from him who is recollected, silence flows like a river.

What does it mean to be recollected? It means to become whole. Silence dwells in a person who is becoming whole. The deeper the wholeness, the deeper the silence.

Who among us is not aching for such silence? But we know, deep down, that there is a mystery to such silence. Such silence is the highest form of communication, and we passionately desire to communicate with God and with one another in this way. But we rationalize silence away because it demands discipline.

Silence is also the fruit of love and cannot be acquired without it. Without love silence is not a pleasant thing. It is aggressive, hostile, imperfect, pushes us away from communication. But when silence comes out of a heart filled with love, then it is the highest form of communication.

Perhaps the first step toward silence is meditation, because we recollect ourselves if we meditate on the words of him whom we love. As we meditate we want to meet the person about whom we are thinking, on whose words we are meditating. Slowly we begin to set the words aside and create within ourselves quiet hearts. We fold the wings of our intellects which up to a point are great disturbers of everything.

Later, much later, we can unfold the wings of the intellect, but up to this point we have to fold them. We must first realize that silence speaks louder than any voices can. Ask lovers, ask married people. They will tell you that there are moments in their lives when words have fallen away like old rags, no longer usable. Love cannot be satisfied with them. Love can only deal with silence.

It's a silence pregnant with God, truly pregnant with God, filled with love. Even between friends, that kind of communicative silence is filled with God. God himself calls us to communication. The Word became incarnate and walked among us and is present now as the Word in our midst. It is this Word that is the real essence of communication.

We go to the Eucharist and receive communion—we communicate with God. He enters into us and becomes part of us. This is accomplished so silently. The hand of a priest gives you a piece of bread and says this is God. The mystery of God meets the mystery of man. It is here that real communication begins. When we are in communication with the Holy Trinity we finally come into communion with all men.

The Silence Within

Monks and nuns, once dedicated to deep and healing silence, seem to have abandoned it. Ordinary men and women living in urban centers, young people pilgrimaging around the world are seeking it. The young people especially are crossing seas and continents to find the key to this silence which is practiced so well by the gurus of the Eastern religions.

For some strange reason, men are feeling the need for silence. But there is no need to cross continents or seas. Silence is truly found within oneself. It is not a mere absence of knowing, but a deep inner silence within, which exists to open a person to the Holy Spirit of the Lord.

Yes, whether men know it or not, they seek that silence so that they can hear God's voice. Men seek that silence so that the two mysteries can meet—the mystery of God's speech to man, and the mystery of man listening to God. Today man is imprisoned in the "I." His mind is turned toward the accumulation of earthly goods or toward some "position" in the world of men. His mind is eternally worried, filled with anxiety and insecurity. Yes, this is the time for silence.

But what is silence? Silence has two faces. One is negation. A man comes into a desert place where no noise penetrates; there is here an impression of emptiness and absence. This face of silence is a waiting, a preparation for dispossession and a strange emptiness.

The other face of silence is one of plenitude. It is an inexpressible state which hides God within its depth. Silence brings, first and foremost, the realization of dispossession. It asks a man to let go of everything and anything that disperses or fragments his true self—anything that cuts him off from God. It invites him to relinquish his useless desires, curiosities and wounds—all the unimportant things that are not of God and which impede his way to him.

Yes, men need and seek Jesus today in a silence that alone allows them to enter their own inner depths and which permits them to shed all the unnecessary possessions accumulated throughout the years.

It is not a matter here of financial or material poverty. No. Interior silence goes much deeper. It is a response to the Christ who says, "Come and follow me into my silence and dispossession from Bethlehem to Nazareth. Come into my hidden life. Leave everything except your true self and follow me."

Silence slowly gives birth to peace within onself. All the clamoring voices that are constantly contradicting one another cease to echo and reecho in the mind and heart. In this calm and silence the Word of the Lord is clearly heard. It is a silence of faith that touches God beyond all words, beyond all ideas, beyond all emotions.

In this silence, reason stays at the threshold, but faith enters fearlessly. Suddenly, in God's own time, faith becomes one with the complete silence of God.

Hope is another dimension of this kind of silence. Hope is rooted in emptiness, in poverty, in a waiting that belongs to the pure of heart. Hopeful silence is patient, thirsty, yet withal dynamic, for it desires to get hold of God—the true Good that is not yet completely ours but will be. In this kind of silence of hope lies our strength.

Silence has a love dimension as well. It is the silence of two people who love each other immensely and passionately and therefore are unable to speak. They enter into the essence of love and are not able to communicate that to anyone else. This silence of the loving soul is an echo of the incredible silence within the Most Holy Trinity.

Yes, men desperately are seeking silence, that kind of silence which once was found in convents and monasteries. Now God, with a lavish generosity, has given this thirst for silence to countless others. By his Spirit may he instruct them in the silent speech of love!

Let's Celebrate!

Celebration is the song of praise coming from the heart of man to the heart of God.

Celebration is the dance of faith that man dances through his whole life—from birth to death—a beautiful dance with its ever-changing pattern that is now intricate, now simple.

Celebration is the expression of hope when men walk in darkness seemingly without anything good nourishing their hope except the dance of faith.

Celebration is love that brings to earth the song of praise—the sound of dancing feet. It is the light that hope sheds in a total darkness.

It is exceedingly important that we extend our hearts to embrace new dimensions of celebration. For usually we think of it as song. We think of it as dance. We think of it as light. We have many ways of thinking about it but, like all spiritual depths, we must not stop before one of its dark or beautiful landscapes. We must go on.

Go on upwards, always upwards, unto the mountain of the Lord, for with every step the life of the spirit embraces wider horizons, acquires new dimensions that we never suspected were there.

In this, the pilgrimage up the holy mountain of the Lord, is what our real spiritual life is all about—climbing to the heights where man, like Moses, meets God almost face to face, or, if at death, then face to face in truth. Yes, we must plunge deeply into that joyful word "celebration," for it contains so much more than what we attribute to it.

Celebration really is a song, a dance, a light, that comes forth from the heart of man when he is totally ready to surrender to God's will and has begun to understand that each new surrender is a cause for greater celebration even though this surrender may lead to pain, to sorrow, to sickness, to loss, as well as to joy and gladness.

Factually, to celebrate means to bring joy and gladness into every step of our lives. Once this new dimension of celebration opens before our eyes, life changes completely, for now we bring to it and into it new ways of helping and serving our brethren in the Lord. By our own celebration of all the events that the will of the Lord brings to us, we give courage and blessing to all we meet.

For who has not met the victim of a terminal disease whom people come to visit in a constant stream. They come to the sickbed to be given the clear notes of a joyous song praising God. Their ears are filled with the dancing feet of the sick one who cannot walk. Into their hands is put a light that has been lighted from the candle of hope, and that dwells in the heart of one who should be hopeless, but isn't.

Yes, the heart of man that celebrates constantly, without ceasing, the will of God and its life is truly equal to a choir that sings Glorias and Alleluias. This chorus should become a clarion call to all who are seeking and not finding, to all who have long ago ceased to sing and who have abandoned any kind of dance.

Come, let us together, hand in hand, climb the mountain of the Lord so that we might understand better what celebration means— and start celebrating!